Evaluating the New Information Technologies

Jerome Johnston, *Editor*

NEW DIRECTIONS FOR PROGRAM EVALUATION
A Publication of the Evaluation Research Society
ERNEST R. HOUSE, *Editor-in-Chief*

Number 23, September 1984

Paperback sourcebooks in
The Jossey-Bass Higher Education and
Social and Behavioral Sciences Series

Jossey-Bass Inc., Publishers
San Francisco • Washington • London

Jerome Johnston, (Ed.).
Evaluating the New Information Technologies.
New Directions for Program Evaluation, no. 23.
San Francisco: Jossey-Bass, 1984.

New Directions for Program Evaluation Series
A Publication of the Evaluation Research Society
Ernest R. House, *Editor-in-Chief*

Copyright © 1984 by Jossey-Bass Inc., Publishers
                and
              Jossey-Bass Limited

Copyright under International, Pan American, and Universal
Copyright Conventions. All rights reserved. No part of
this issue may be reproduced in any form — except for brief
quotation (not to exceed 500 words) in a review or professional
work — without permission in writing from the publishers.

New Directions for Program Evaluation (publication number
USPS 449-050) is published quarterly by Jossey-Bass Inc.,
Publishers, and is sponsored by the Evaluation Research Society.
Second-class postage rates paid at San Francisco, California,
and at additional mailing offices.

Correspondence:
Subscriptions, single-issue orders, change of address notices, undelivered
copies, and other correspondence should be sent to Subscriptions,
Jossey-Bass Inc., Publishers, 433 California Street, San Francisco
California 94104.

Editorial correspondence should be sent to the Editor-in-Chief,
Ernest House, CIRCE-270, Education Building, University of Illinois,
Champaign, Ill. 61820.

Library of Congress Catalogue Card Number LC 83-82737
International Standard Serial Number ISSN 0164-7989
International Standard Book Number ISBN 87589-784-3

Cover art by Willi Baum
Manufactured in the United States of America

Ordering Information

The paperback sourcebooks listed below are published quarterly and can be ordered either by subscription or single-copy.

Subscriptions cost $35.00 per year for institutions, agencies, and libraries. Individuals can subscribe at the special rate of $25.00 per year *if payment is by personal check*. (Note that the full rate of $35.00 applies if payment is by institutional check, even if the subscription is designated for an individual.) Standing orders are accepted. Subscriptions normally begin with the first of the four sourcebooks in the current publication year of the series. When ordering, please indicate if you prefer your subscription to begin with the first issue of the *coming* year.

Single copies are available at $8.95 when payment accompanies order, and *all single-copy orders under $25.00 must include payment*. (California, New Jersey, New York, and Washington, D.C., residents please include appropriate sales tax.) For billed orders, cost per copy is $8.95 plus postage and handling. (Prices subject to change without notice.)

Bulk orders (ten or more copies) of any individual sourcebook are available at the following discounted prices: 10-49 copies, $8.05 each; 50-100 copies, $7.15 each; over 100 copies, *inquire*. Sales tax and postage and handling charges apply as for single copy orders.

To ensure correct and prompt delivery, all orders must give either the *name of an individual* or an *official purchase order number*. Please submit your order as follows:

Subscriptions: specify series and year subscription is to begin.
Single Copies: specify sourcebook code (such as, PE8) and first two words of title.

Mail orders for United States and Possessions, Latin America, Canada, Japan, Australia, and New Zealand to:
 Jossey-Bass Inc., Publishers
 433 California Street
 San Francisco, California 94104

Mail orders for all other parts of the world to:
 Jossey-Bass Limited
 28 Banner Street
 London EC1Y 8QE

New Directions for Program Evaluation Series
Ernest R. House, *Editor-in-Chief*

PE1 *Exploring Purposes and Dimensions,* Scarvia B. Anderson, Claire D. Coles
PE2 *Evaluating Federally Sponsored Programs,* Charlotte C. Rentz, R. Robert Rentz
PE3 *Monitoring Ongoing Programs,* Donald L. Grant
PE4 *Secondary Analysis,* Robert F. Boruch
PE5 *Utilization of Evaluative Information,* Larry A. Braskamp, Robert D. Brown

PE6 *Measuring the Hard-to-Measure,* Edward H. Loveland
PE7 *Values, Ethics, and Standards in Evaluation,* Robert Perloff, Evelyn Perloff
PE8 *Training Program Evaluators,* Lee Sechrest
PE9 *Assessing and Interpreting Outcomes,* Samuel Ball
PE10 *Evaluation of Complex Systems,* Ronald J. Wooldridge
PE11 *Measuring Effectiveness,* Dan Baugher
PE12 *Federal Efforts to Develop New Evaluation Methods,* Nick L. Smith
PE13 *Field Assessments of Innovative Evaluation Methods,* Nick L. Smith
PE14 *Making Evaluation Research Useful to Congress,* Leonard Saxe, Daniel Koretz
PE15 *Standards for Evaluation Practice,* Peter H. Rossi
PE16 *Applications of Time Series Analysis to Evaluation,* Garlie A. Forehand
PE17 *Stakeholder-Based Evaluation,* Anthony S. Bryk
PE18 *Management and Organization of Program Evaluation,* Robert G. St.Pierre
PE19 *Philosophy of Evaluation,* Ernest R. House
PE20 *Developing Effective Internal Evaluation,* Arnold J. Love
PE21 *Making Effective Use of Mailed Questionnaires,* Daniel C. Lockhart
PE22 *Secondary Analysis of Available Data Bases,* David J. Bowering

Contents

Editor's Notes 1
Jerome Johnston

Chapter 1. Videotex for Market Information: 5
A Survey of Prototype Users
James S. Ettema

Videotex is a new technology in search of a market. Formative evaluation of a prototype system can help developers to refine a product and define a market. A survey of adopters and nonadopters of a prototype videotex system, when coupled with machine-collected data about system usage, provided rich information for that purpose.

Chapter 2. Teletext for Public Information: Laboratory 23
and Field Studies
Martin Elton, John Carey

Teletext is another technology searching for a market. A series of laboratory and field studies provided useful information in this regard, and the researchers' experience is a primer on how to conduct field research in natural settings.

Chapter 3. Microcomputers in Schools: The Video Case Study 43
as an Evaluation Tool
Henry T. Ingle

When a technological innovation is driven by market-push forces and the innovation is itself rapidly evolving, the video case study is an efficient vehicle for the collection and dissemination of evaluation data. It provides snapshots of usage that allow others to see for themselves what happens among early adopters and to make value judgments of their own.

Chapter 4. Evaluating New Media Systems 53
Ronald E. Rice

New media, such as electronic mail and word processing, are playing increasingly important roles in communication activities, especially in organizational settings. The complex communication tasks that they are designed to facilitate demand theory-driven conceptualization and innovative approaches to research about them. Several recent studies provide guidance.

Chapter 5. Research Methods for Evaluating the New 73
Information Technologies
Jerome Johnston

When applied to the new technologies, many concepts and research strategies of program evaluation require some adaptation. The newness and instability of the technologies, the complex ways in which they fit into existing patterns of human behavior, and their novelty to most users suggest new strategies for both formative and summative evaluation activities.

Index

Editor's Notes

In recent years, new devices for information retrieval, management, and exchange have proliferated. Currently, these devices include microcomputers, videodisc, videotex, teletext, and electronic mail. Many more innovations can be expected in the coming months and years.

Product developers, potential consumers, and those interested in the organizational and societal payoff of these new technologies need evaluations of them. How can these evaluations best be done? Will traditional approaches provide the necessary information? This *New Directions for Program Evaluation* sourcebook describes and assesses the research approaches that social scientists have used in recent studies of new technologies. The methodologies include traditional user surveys, case studies, and analysis of user data generated by the technologies themselves. In addition, the authors recount their research findings and provide some early reports on the utility of the new technologies for various purposes.

In a technology-push model, which applies to new technologies in the information arena, a needs assessment has limited utility. Most of the new technologies have an intrinsic fascination for consumers, not so much because they accomplish burdensome tasks more easily than traditional methods do but because consumers are fascinated with the breathtaking speed and elegance with which the machines operate, whether the speed is important or not. People have gotten by quite well without many of the functions that they provide. Needs assessments of naive populations may be able to identify some wants that technology's developers can exploit, but a carefully selected market segment must be defined if there is to be hope that a set of true needs can be uncovered. One way of assessing the viability of a market is to offer a prototype product and compare the characteristics of those who adopt it with the characteristics of those who do not. James Ettema used this strategy for the concept-testing portion of his study of videotex, which he describes in Chapter One.

The challenge in assessing the features and impact of the new technologies lies in their very newness. If evaluation is defined at least in part as the collection of information about the impact of an intervention, then the new technologies present a real challenge to evaluators. The users themselves have limited experience. For that reason, some useful evaluative information can be obtained by examining the users of prototype systems. Ettema's examination in Chapter One of a prototype videotex system designed for agricultural market information provides a good example of such a study. Ettema's research shows how a single study can meet the needs of both product developers and society at large. The survey instrument was developed to get user feedback on machine-specific characteristics. Drawing on a large communications literature on information needs and benefits, the survey instrument was also able to assess the fit of videotex to the information needs of a narrow market of potential users.

To identify how the prototype test market used the technology, Ettema relied on the "new data" made possible by microprocessor-based technologies. His data on user behaviors were collected by the very machines under study. Such an approach is very appealing, because it obviates the need for a questionnaire. However, Ettema's experience also highlights the difficulties in using such data.

Teletext, another of the new technologies, enables users to display "pages" or frames of text and graphic information on a television set. Martin Elton and John Carey orchestrated a number of laboratory and field studies designed to provide a variety of stakeholders with information about the utility of teletext for public service information. In Chapter Two, Elton and Carey analyze the strengths and weaknesses of laboratory and field studies in assessing the advantages of new and changing technology. The details that they provide will be illuminating to anyone who is considering this research approach. They make a compelling case in favor of field studies and illustrate the advantages of multiple measures in such research.

Schools are under increasing pressure from parents and the media to expand the use of microcomputers in the classroom. The pressure seems fueled more by the hope of valuable educational benefits than by hard evidence, which is hard to come by. Computers are being used in many different ways: for drill-and-practice, programming, and word processing, to name only a few. The hardware and software are changing so rapidly that evaluations cannot be conducted on any particular configuration, because the chances are that it will have been superseded by the time the evaluation results are ready. In such a situation, decision makers desiring guidance can be helped by snapshots of how early adopters are using microcomputers and by hearing teachers and administrators tell their stories and express their judgments. Videotape case studies can provide such information. In Chapter Three, Henry Ingle aruges in favor of video case studies. He describes how his Project BEST team sought to overlay the art of filmmaking with the discipline of social science both in taping the original case studies and in assembling an edited version that synthesized and illustrated the lessons of the individual case studies.

Business settings are rapidly adopting and adapting the new information technologies to work settings. Here, such innovations as word processing, electronic messaging, and computer conferencing are prominent. Reflecting his roots in the field of communication, Ronald Rice calls these innovations *new media*. In Chapter Four, he argues that good theory is useful in designing technology evaluations. Rice provides illustrations of the contribution of theoretical constructs to a number of evaluations, including several of his own. He cites adoption studies that draw on the diffusion of innovation literature; usage studies that incorporate media style variables; and organizational impact studies that draw on social presence and network analysis theory. Theory, he argues persuasively, deepens the insights that evaluations provide. Rice makes a number of useful methodological recommendations, including using the so-called "new data" — computer-monitored data on user behaviors.

Are the traditional paradigms of program evaluation appropriate for the study of information technology? In Chapter Five, Jerome Johnston considers this question. He notes that many evaluation strategies were developed originally to help shape new educational products or assess the impact of educational programs. The communication activity promoted by the new technologies is different from classroom learning, and the differences affect the usefulness of traditional evaluation strategies for the study of new technologies. The formative evaluation paradigm used to develop linear educational products is not well suited to the shaping of interactive products. The summative evaluation paradigm rests on well-developed theories of educational growth and change, but theories regarding technology and change are not as refined.

In the absence of good theories, we must rely on laboratory studies and field trials in which evaluators can observe and speculate on the many ways in which a technology interacts with and changes humans and their context. In measurement, the paper-and-pencil survey must be supplemented with other methods, especially naturalistic observation and case studies. Finally, the conduct of good evaluation requires time — time for subjects to become familiar with the intervention or be affected by it and time to collect, analyze, and report data. For evaluation to be useful when technologies are evolving so rapidly, evaluators must figure out how to shorten the time required.

Jerome Johnston
Editor

Jerome Johnston is associate research scientist at the Institute for Social Research at the University of Michigan. For the last eight years, his research has focused on the development and impact of educational television. His publications include tests of television's effects, policy studies of television's utility, and examinations of methods used to study television.

This overview of results from the field trial of a prototype information system examines issues of concern to both the system developer and society as a whole.

Videotex for Market Information: A Survey of Prototype Users

James S. Ettema

Enticing promises have been made for new information technologies, such as videotex. For potential developers of videotex services, there has been the promise of new businesses (Compaine, 1981; Robinson, 1982; Sigel, 1983; Smith, 1980). For society as a whole, the technology promises enhanced and equalized access to information for citizens and increased productivity in both public and private enterprise (Chen, 1977; Martin and Norman, 1970).

An opportunity to evaluate the ability of videotex to fulfill such promises was recently provided by the First Bank System, a Minneapolis-based bank holding company, which opened its prototype agricultural videotex system, FirstHand, to examination by the author and colleagues. The evaluation, sponsored by the National Science Foundation, sought to define and address the social issues raised by technology. Throughout the project, society was seen as a primary stakeholder in the evaluation. At the same time, the evaluation could not ignore issues of interest to the developer. After all, a commitment to

The research reported in this chapter was supported by the Information Impact Program, Division of Information Science and Technology, National Science Foundation, under grant IST-8212164.

private development of information technology makes it unlikely that the promises to society can be fulfilled unless the promises to developers are also fulfilled. The evaluation thus sought to examine the societal-level impact in a way that promotes beneficial and socially responsible development of the technology. This overview of the project highlights the notion that developer and society are both stakeholders in the evaluation.

The Developer's Stake: The Technology and Its Market

For the would-be system developer, the problem is one of developing the technology into a profitable enterprise. Thus, the developer is interested in data that can help to define both the potential market and the technology itself. Technical attributes alone do not determine the nature of technology as product. The social and economic role of videotex technology must be defined in the marketplace, just as television technology was defined (Williams, 1975). At the same time, the current wants and needs of potential users do not completely determine the market for a service. To some extent, both wants and needs can be created and controlled. Thus, both the particular configuration of a given technology and the demand of particular market segments must be created and recreated until a profitable match is achieved.

For these reasons, a would-be developer who needs definitions of technology and market has to make some assumptions about both, then develop a prototype system and test it on a particular market segment. First Bank System chose to develop a prototype system for a market segment composed of the operators of relatively large farms, both because agriculture is important to its service area and because that particular market segment overlaps with others of interest, such as small business and middle- and upper-income consumers.

Substantial research went into conceptualization of the prototype system. In response to changes in the competitive environment brought about the Monetary Deregulation and Control Act of 1980, the First Bank System undertook a study of alternative banking service delivery systems, such as automated teller machines and home banking networks. The idea for FirstHand emerged from this study and from several subsequent studies, which indicated that home banking would be of interest particularly to dual-income families. However, a viable system would require more than banking services; thus, any system would need to be designed to meet the nonbanking needs and interests of a particular market segment.

For the study of FirstHand, operators of moderate to large

farms around three North Dakota communities—Fargo, Valley City, and Wahpeton—were recruited. To be eligible for participation, farm operators had to meet a number of criteria, including minimum farm size and income. Participants were provided with the small French videotex terminals. They could access the host computers through Tymnet simply by making a local telephone call to a node in their community.

FirstHand offered five kinds of informational and transactional services: agricultural market data; agricultural product information; news, weather, and sports; home and family information; and transactional services. Regional and national commodity prices, along with market analysis and forecasts, were provided by AGRI-DATA, a commercial agricultural information broker. Crop and livestock production information was provided by the Agricultural Extension Division of North Dakota State University (NDSU). National, state, and local news, weather, and sports edited for an agricultural audience were provided by the Fargo *Forum* newspaper, and newspapers in Wahpeton and Valley City provided news from their communities. Health, homemaking, and other family information was provided by several information sources, including the Pillsbury Company and NDSU's Extension Division. Finally, advertising and sale information was provided by a number of local and regional retailers, and a subset of system users could use it to order from the J. C. Penney catalogue. Funds transfer and accounting services were provided by local affiliates of the First Bank System. Like the home shopping service, this service was available only to a subset of users.

It is ironic that, owing to the complexity of the software required and other factors, home banking, which spurred the development of the system as a whole, was the least well developed of the services offered to prototype users. FirstHand thus provides only a very limited test of videotex for home banking and other transactional services. The information services were much more fully developed, although they were not completely without technical problems, and information was sometimes slow to be updated. Nevertheless, FirstHand provides a reasonably good test of videotex for information retrieval.

The FirstHand system is of particular interest because it allows us to examine and test some current theorizing about the suitability of videotex to various information applications. For example, it has been argued that the future of interactive systems lies in the delivery of highly perishable data, not in the storage and retrieval of relatively timeless knowledge (Kline and Clarke, 1978). It has also been argued that the future lies in specialized technical, professional, or business information, not in consumer information of general interest (Carey, 1982; Sigel,

1983). As it happens, FirstHand's array of informational services neatly embodies these distinctions: The farm market data service offers highly perishable business data, while the home and family information service offers much less perishable information of personal interest. Ratings of importance attached to these various types of information and participant's actual use of and expressed satisfaction with information services of FirstHand can help the developer to work out practical yet conceptually based definitions of both the technology and its market.

The logic of a field trial is to make a best guess about the technology and its market, develop a prototype product, and study the responses to that product. Two general sorts of response are useful to the developer in defining the technology and the market: first, the response of the chosen market segment to the system and services as concepts; second, the response of users to the prototype system and services.

The response of the market to the system as a concept can help to answer three questions. First, who in the potential market is interested in the system enough to become a user? The marketing research on consumer-oriented systems that Dozier and Rice (forthcoming) have reviewed indicates that early adopters are of higher socioeconomic status, younger, and heavier users of other media. In the case of FirstHand, which combines consumer and business services, it is reasonable to expect that business characteristics, such as size of farming operation, will also help to define potential users.

Second, what are the current information wants and needs of the market? Communication research suggests that self-defined information needs are often better predictors of communication behavior than demographics are (Dervin, 1980; Ettema and Kline, 1977). Thus, the match between the information desired by potential users and the information offered by a system can predict adoption of the system. Of course, the information needs of potential users can also help to refine the array of services that the system offers.

Third, what criteria do adopters use in making the decision to adopt the system? A variety of criteria besides unmet information needs must influence the decision. Perceived consumer and business benefits as well as perceived problems in using the system are likely to be among these criteria (Dozier and Rice, forthcoming; Dozier and Ledingham, 1982).

Those who choose to become users of the prototype system can help to answer three other questions. First, what problems did they actually encounter in using the system? Problems can be ergonomic; for example, there may be flaws in the design of the terminal, or there may be other hardware-related problems. The problems can also include content; for example, information may be slow to be updated, or complex interactions between system, contents, and user may make it difficult for a user to find the information desired.

Second, how much is the system and, more important, each of its individual services actually used? For the system developer, who will have a profitable system only if the system is used, data on actual usage is the bottom line. However, these data can be misleading early in the development of a technology and its market. Comparative data on usage levels of individual services may be both more meaningful and quite useful in refining the array of services offered.

Third, how do users themselves evaluate the system and its services? Actual use may be the bottom line, but user evaluations will be valuable in diagnosing the strengths and weaknesses of the system. Satisfaction ratings may have some value, but an exploration of the particular benefits obtained from the system will also be highly useful. Further, the notion that the system should be developed to meet the needs of users as they themselves define those needs shifts attention from mean ratings of overall satisfaction to the relationship between information needs and the satisfaction of particular needs. Thus, the value of the system to users can be established by showing that those who report needs also report benefits that help to satisfy those needs. After all, it is unlikely that an information system will be used very widely if it does not meet the needs of users as they define those needs.

Society's Stake: Social Impact

Society's stake in evaluation is the opportunity that it gives us for an early reading—perhaps also a projection—of the social consequences of a given technology. One possible consequence is enhanced access to information, and that in turn may enhance productivity. The new information systems promise users access to vast libraries of up-to-the-minute information, which can be retrieved with great speed and precision; that is, a high percentage of the items retrieved by information seekers are judged to be relevant or correct. Thus, users can quickly retrieve a specific item of desired information (such as the current price of a specific commodity in a particular market) from a huge and constantly updated data base (such as the prices of all commodities in all markets). It is this promise of information easily obtained that supports the promise of increased productivity in business and other enterprises.

The question of enhanced access to information raised on behalf of society can be addressed with the same data that interests the developer. Both stakeholders are interested in the benefits that the system can actually provide and in the relationship between information needs and the benefits obtained. From the developer's point of view, the fit between the information needs and the benefits obtained is a question of the system's value to potential customers, but from society's point of view, it is a question of the ability of technology to enhance productivity. Productivity can be enhanced only when real needs are met. But, the desirable social consequence of enhanced productivity can conflict with another desirable consequence: information equity. The notion of examining the relationship between self-reported information needs and benefits received from the system presupposes that neither needs nor benefits are uniformly distributed within society. Some users are better served than others, because they have the sorts of problems that the technology of a particular application is most able to solve. The technology of a particular application thus interacts with the needs of potential users to enhance the productivity of some more than others, and it thereby creates inequities.

It is important to understand that inequities do not begin with the differences among users in benefits obtained. Indeed, there are at least two earlier stages in the development of information inequities. The first stage involves the choice of certain social groups as the potential market. Most existing electronic information systems have been created to serve the needs of professions, such as law and medicine, or of individuals in other highly specialized and technical work. Other groups, such as upscale urbanites, have been chosen as the market for systems now under development. But, some groups may never be chosen. At the first stage, then, the question of information equity is, For whom have information systems been developed? For FirstHand, it was not merely farmers but moderate to large farmers who were also bank customers.

At the next stage, society's question of information equity converges with the developer's question of who is interested in the system; but, while the developer sees the question as one of defining the target market, society sees it as one of equity in the diffusion of the innovation. The introduction of an innovation more often widens than narrows the gap between haves and have-nots, and there is little reason to believe that the introduction of an innovation in information delivery will not widen the gap between information haves and have-nots (Paisley, 1980). Katzman (1974) argues that the gaps between early and late adopters of a particular innovation often do close, but by the time they do, the early adopters have gone on to something else. Thus, while both the developer and society in general have an interest in early adopters, those interests do not entirely coincide. Developers need to begin the diffusion process somewhere, while society has an interest in minimizing the gap between information haves and have-nots.

Only after facing the questions of differential development and differential adoption do we come to the question of differential benefit. At this third stage, the question is, Who within the actual group of users benefits most from the system? Correlations between benefit measures and information need measures indicate more effective information seeking and perhaps enhanced productivity. However, correlations between benefit measures and such demographics as farm size indicate inequities. Thus, there is likely to be tension between productivity and equity at all three stages. Society's stake is to find some balance between the consequences of enhanced productivity and intensified inequity. It is important to monitor the balance struck by information technology in general and by specific information systems in particular.

Design and Method of the Evaluation

The issues raised on behalf of both stakeholders are addressed with data drawn from two sources. One source was made possible by the technology: The system's own computers kept records of system use during several periods near the middle and end of the eight-month trial. These records were aggregated to obtain three measures: total time spent by each user in each service, total number of sign-ons to each service, and total number of pages accessed within each service. Total time spent by users in each service was chosen as the single best measure of use, because it was thought to be more sensitive to intentional, purposeful use than total sign-ons and less sensitive to search errors (that is, pages accessed by mistake) than pages accessed. However, these three measures were strongly intercorrelated ($r = .79$ to $.97$), although they were much less strongly correlated with self-reported use ($r = .33$ to $.39$). Thus, it is less important which of the system-monitored measures is used than that a system-monitored rather than a self-reported measure is used. The other source of the data reported here was a mail survey conducted near the end of the field trial.

Respondents were divided into groups for analysis. For questions concerning who adopts the system and why, a sample of nonadopters (farm operators approached by the First Bank System who declined to participate) was compared with a sample of adopters (farm operators who agreed to participate). Comparisons of demographic characteristics, information needs, and the importance of various criteria in the adoption decision for adopters and nonadopters all reflect on the adoption process as an issue of both marketing and social impact. For analysis of user response to the system and services, the adopter group is further divided into those who participated in the field trial and those who did not; there were not enough terminals for all those who were interested. The reports of system users concerning problems encountered and benefits obtained reflect on the value of the system to potential customers. A demographic analysis of who benefits reflects on the social issue of information equity. The response rate for the mail questionnaire was 72 percent. This resulted in a nonadopter group composed of 104 respondents and an adopter group of 225 of which 139 were system users.

This "one shot" survey was designed to gain information on as many different issues as possible. Of course, the method is subject to the usual problems of retrospective self-reports. The method precludes a demonstration of change in knowledge or other such outcomes. An attempt to demonstrate a limited number of outcomes, such as knowledge gain, experimentally was rejected in favor of sounding out users on benefits and other outcomes via self-reports. Thus, the project described here was intended less to demonstrate the value or lack of value of the system than to explore some possibilities.

Response to the System as Concept

Who is interested in the system enough to become a user? The question of who responds favorably to a system as a concept is an issue of both marketing and societal concern. In the FirstHand study, the issue was addressed by comparing adopters and nonadopters on key demographic characteristics. These comparisons offer few surprises to anyone familiar with the diffusion of innovations. Adopters were younger and better educated than nonadopters, although their family incomes were not larger on the average. Adopters had somewhat larger farms than nonadopters, in terms of both income and acres planted in cash crops. However, the biggest difference was that adopters' farms employed substantially more agricultural innovations of all sorts than did the farms of nonadopters. Thus, the most powerful discriminator between adopters and nonadopters — innovations employed — is a characteristic of the farm, but at the same time it clearly reflects a characteristic of the farm operation — a generalized willingness to innovate. It is less the mere presence of resources, such as a large farm or a good education, than the deployment of those resources that determines willingness to experiment with technology.

What are the current information wants and needs of the market?

Personal and farm characteristics are likely to be reflected in the farm operators' needs for information, and the information needs are likely to be reflected in farmers' interest in a new information system. To assess these information wants and needs, both adopters and nonadopters were asked to rate the importance of four categories of information, corresponding to FirstHand's four main information services; farm market data, farm production information, news, and home and family information. In addition, they were asked to rate their level of satisfaction with existing sources for these sorts of information.

Results show that both adopters and nonadopters rated market data as by far the most important of the four categories of information, and they rated home and family information as the least important. However, both groups were less satisfied with existing sources for both market data and home and family information than they were with existing sources for the other categories of information. Results also show that three of the four importance ratings discriminated significantly between adopters and nonadopters but still less powerfully than most of the demographics did. Adopters rated market data as more important than nonadopters did, and they rated news and family information as less important than nonadopters did. The ratings of satisfaction with existing information services did not discriminate at all, indicating that adopters were not particularly motivated by dissatisfaction with existing information sources.

Altogether, these results suggest that information need is not an undifferentiated concept. Importance ratings vary greatly across four information topics. More than that, however, market data are more valued by adopters, while news and home and family information are more valued by nonadopters. Satisfaction with existing sources of information also varies somewhat across topics, although adopters are neither more nor less satisfied than nonadopters are. Thus, while demographic analysis may suggest generalized innovativeness as a determinant of adoption, there is no corresponding generalized information need or want that motivates adoption. This conclusion is also supported by the finding that adopters and nonadopters differed very little in their use of other informational media.

These results also suggest that the role of information needs in an adoption decision is not a simple one. Adopters did report, via the importance ratings, a greater need for market data than the nonadopters did. The adopters also reported, via the satisfaction ratings of existing market data sources, that their needs for such information were not being met as well as they might have been. However, adopters were not less satisfied with existing sources of this information than nonadopters were, which indicates that dissatisfaction with existing information sources was not very important in the decision to adopt the system.

What criteria do adopters use in making the decision to adopt the system? To give us more information about the adoption decision, we asked respondents about their criteria for that decision. Comparisons of the importance that adopters and nonadopters assigned to various criteria show that desire for market data powerfully motivated the decision to adopt the system. Adopters were also impressed by the promise of general farm-related benefits, such as getting better prices for commodities and making better farming decisions. It is worth noting in this regard that, in a factor analysis of all the decision criteria, the desire for market data, together with the farm-related benefit items, defined the first factor. Thus, the marketing information that the system promised was intimately bound up with the promise of general farm-related benefits.

Several perceived drawbacks to the system played a part in the decision of nonadopters. There was concern about learning to use the technology. Two demographic charcteristics, farm size and proximity to retirement, were other important criteria in the decision not to adopt. Many farmers felt that their operation was too small or that they were too close to retirement to bother with this innovation.

Overall, it is clear that the adoption decision turned heavily on the desire for market data, which was seen to be of general farm benefit. Although the importance ratings and the satisfaction ratings do not unequivocally show an unmet need for market data among adopters, the decision criteria clearly show a desire for it among adopters.

Response to the System in Prototype

What problems did users encounter with the system? Users rated the severity of numerous possible problems with FirstHand. Results show that the design of the terminals was not much of a problem for users. Readability of the screen was almost never a problem for users, nor was the size or the shape of the keys. Two other features of the system's design, however, did pose some problems. The absence of a printer was rated as occasionally a problem and the need for a modem, which tied up the telephone during system use, was rated as one of the greatest problems with the system. Several problems related to software, such as inability to find the desired information, also emerged as a severe problem, but even the most severe problems were rated as less than often a problem. A factor analysis of the problems did not yield well-defined factors, which suggests that particular combinations of problems were user-specific, not general.

In further analyses, problems were correlated with use of the system and benefits obtained from it. The pattern of correlations suggested that problems with the system could be placed into two categories, hindrances and nuisances. Hindrances—for example, problems in locating desired information—are negatively correlated with use and benefit. Those who experience these problems may tend to use the system less, and they benefit less as a result. However, nuisances—for example, the lack of a printer—are positively correlated with use and benefit. Why? It seems unlikely that nuisance-type problems in any way enhance use or benefit. Rather, it seems likely that those who use the system more and benefit from it find such problems nuisances. Thus, problems with this technology may vary not only in their severity but also in their causal relationship to use and benefit.

How much is the system used? Actual use of the system in the bottom line for the developer, at least in the short run. Usage records show that the market data service—the most heavily used of the four services—was used slightly less than three minutes a week on the average. It is important to place this average within the context of the great variation observed across users. While use of the market data service averaged about three minutes a week, the standard deviation was more than four minutes a week. Similarly, the standard deviations for the other services were large compared to the means. A good deal of this variation results from the fact that a number of farmers who had the system did not use it. More than one fifth of those with access to the system never signed on to the market data service, while more than one half never signed on to the production information service.

It is also important to recognize that the usage data are for an experimental system. Thus, we need to focus less on comparing levels of use of the new services with levels of use of other, more familiar media than we do on comparing use of the individual services. The usage data clearly differentiate among the services offered. Not surprisingly, the market data service that motivated adoption of the system was the service most used. However, the news service, which had more interest for nonadopters than it did for adopters, was a strong second in terms of actual use. Use of the home and family information service was third, and use of the production information service was a distant and surprising fourth—essentially, it was not used. Overall, it seems that FirstHand was used more for brief periods to monitor fast-changing information, such as commodity prices and news, than for extended periods to retrieve less perishable information, such as recipes and crop information.

How do users evaluate the system? Satisfaction with the various services is one outcome of particular interest to the system developer. Indeed, the FirstHand developer devoted much of its own survey of users to this outcome. Results indicated, however, that satisfaction ratings did not differentiate among the four services offered. Ratings for all four services clustered around the somewhat satisfied level.

Comparison of these ratings with the satisfaction ratings for other sources of information is more instructive. Satisfaction with other news sources is quite high, and the rating of the FirstHand news service falls far short of that level. In contrast, the satisfaction with other market data sources was quite low, and the rating of the FirstHand service exceeds it slightly. Ratings of other sources of production information and of home and family information are about the same as the ratings given to corresponding FirstHand services. Altogether, then, these results suggest that users judge the news service to fall far short of existing news sources and the market data service to be a little better than existing sources. The other information services provided by the system are neither better nor worse than existing sources.

The vagueness of the concept of user satisfaction prompted us to explore what users actually got out of the system. This exploration focused primarily on productivity-related benefits. We asked users to rate the system on a variety of productivity dimensions. A factor analysis of these ratings produced three intercorrelated factors. The first factor was labeled *general benefit*, because the items that loaded most heavily on it included the most general productivity-related benefits (for example, usefulness of the system in saving time and energy, in making better decisions, and in keeping better informed in general) as well as several benefits related specifically to farm commodity marketing (for example, usefulness of the system in making decisions about marketing and in keeping up to date on markets). The second factor was labeled *information-seeking value*, because it included such items as the value of the system in saving time and energy by bringing various kinds of information together in one place, by making information quickly available whenever it was needed, and by allowing the selection of only the information desired. The third factor, labeled *decision-making value*, included such items as the usefulness of the system in making decisions more quickly and in making decisions in a more organized and rational way.

When the items that loaded the most heavily on each factor were averaged to create three indexes of benefits obtained, the information-seeking value index emerged with the highest average—somewhat useful. The decision-making value index emerged with the lowest average—slightly useful. The general benefit index was about halfway between. This result clearly reflects the fact that the system was an informational medium for large-scale farmers in general, not a decision-support system that could be tailored to each farmer's individual needs.

These average benefit ratings suggest that the system was something less than indispensible. However, several bivariate analyses involving the ratings suggest that the system had real value. Results here show significant and positive if modest ($r = .25$ to $.30$) correlations between the three benefit indexes and an information-need index. Thus, those who most wanted information were more likely to say that they got it from the system. This outcome is positive both for the developer, who must create a product of value, and for society, which must monitor the contribution that information technology makes to productivity.

Another interesting if somewhat surprising finding related to users' information needs: use of both newspapers and radio—two important sources of agricultural information—was significantly and negatively related to the benefit indexes. Those who use the other media less reported greater benefits from FirstHand. This result, too, can be interpreted as an indication that the system has real information value. Perhaps because the system brought various kinds of information together in one place and offered other features that helped users to save time and energy, it did help to meet a need that other, traditional media did not serve well.

Still another set of important bivariate relationships—those of particular interest to society as stakeholder—involve the relationships between benefit measures and demographic measures. These relationships bear on the question of equity in the distribution of benefits, and the results raise some equity concerns. Farmers who reported greater benefits from the system tended clearly to be younger, better educated, and more innovative. However, personal income was negatively related to reported benefit, and farm income was not related at all. Thus, it seems to be not so much the large and well-to-do farmers who benefit as it does young farmers on their way up.

Implications for Stakeholders

For the developer, this evaluation helps to define both the technology itself and the market for it. A definition of the technology is suggested by responses to the FirstHand videotex system both as a concept (comparing the response of adopters with those of nonadopters) and in prototype (examining the responses of users). When the responses to the four types of information and the four corresponding FirstHand information services are sorted into the four cells of the matrix shown in Figure 1, the pattern suggests that farmers defined FirstHand primarily as a way of remaining up-to-date on information that is of business rather than of personal interest and that is more rather than less perishable. Interest in highly perishable business information (market data) seemed to motivate the adoption decision, and the service that provided such information was the most favorably received, as measured by both satisfaction and actual use. Thus, the evaluation reported here defined FirstHand more as a technologically up-to-date tickertape than as an electronic library.

Given that FirstHand was defined primarily as a high-speed

Figure 1. Matrix of Responses to the Information in FirstHand

	More-Perishable Information	*Less-Perishable Information*
	Farm Market Data	*Agricultural Production*
Business Information	*Response to Concept* *Rated as most important information by all respondents *Rated as more important by adopters than by nonadopters *Most wanted service among adopters *Response to Prototype* *Users slightly more satisfied with this service than with preexisting sources *Most heavily used service	*Response to Concept* *Rated as second most important information by all respondents *Rated as equally important by adopters and nonadopters *Response to Prototype* *Users no more satisfied with this service than with preexisting sources *Least heavily used service
	General News	*Home and Family*
Consumer Information	*Response to Concept* *Rated as third most important information by all respondents *Rated as less important by adopters than by nonadopters *Least wanted service among adopters *Response to Prototype* *Users much less satisfied with this service than with preexisting sources *Second most heavily used service	*Response to Concept* *Rated as least important information by all respondents *Rated as less important by adopters than by nonadopters *Response to Prototype* *Users no more satisfied with this service than with preexisting sources *Third most heavily used service

delivery system for agricultural market data, a definition of the emerging market for this new technology is suggested by those who responded positively to the system as a concept. The early adopters of this innovation were much like the adopters of other agricultural innovations: They were younger and better educated, and their farms were larger and, most notably, more innovative. It is also clear that the adopters wanted the system for the farm market data that it promised to deliver. It is not clear, however, that these farmers had an urgent need for this particular innovation. Adopters did rate farm market information as more important than nonadopters did, but they expressed no less satisfaction with preexisting sources than nonadopters did. Further, data on use of other media indicate that adopters were not much heavier information seekers than nonadopters. Thus, videotex system developers may be in a situation similar to that of home computers makers: Their products may be needed less than they are wanted. Diffusion may have to be driven more by marketer push than by market pull.

The response of users to the system in actual prototype suggests that this particular system, perhaps, also the technology in general, has far to go before it becomes critical to farming success. Problems with the system, while not severe, did seem to hinder its effective use somewhat, and even the most heavily used of the services was not used extensively compared with other media. Further, users rated even the most beneficial aspects of the system as something less than indispensible.

However, other results suggest that the system could have real value for users. For example, the measures of benefits obtained were correlated with the measures of benefits most desired by adopters. The interpretation here is that an information need—or at least a want—is being met. Further, those who used the traditional media less tended also to report greater benefit from their use of FirstHand. Thus, the system may have real value for those with little time or opportunity to use other, traditional media. This suggests that the system, perhaps as a result of its technological attributes, may fill a market niche that other media do not already occupy.

Both society in general and individual users have a stake in the system's benefits. The correlations between the information-need measure and the benefit indexes suggest that the system can enhance information-seeking efficiency and perhaps farm productivity as well. Beyond the mere existence of benefit, the key social issue is the distribution of benefit. The distribution of benefit—that is, information equity—should be examined at three levels. At the first level, a concern for information equity directs attention to the question of which social groups a particular information system serves. The history of FirstHand's development reveals both the importance of the question (the developer deliberately set out to create a system for some users and not for others) and the answer to that question (for FirstHand, the users were defined as the operators of moderate to large farms).

At the next level, a concern for information equity directs attention to diffusion of the system. The profile of FirstHand's early adopters resembled the profile of early adopters for other innovations. It is important to acknowledge that typical diffusion is unequal diffusion. Command of such resources as education, land, and income affected who adopted the FirstHand technology. However, the demographic characteristics were eclipsed by innovativeness and by the desire, if not the need, for information of a particular type. Thus, farmers' receptivity to this technology was influenced more by their orientation to the technology than by their resources.

Some of the same characteristics of farm and farmer are also influential at the third level of the information equity issue. This level directs attention to the distribution of benefits among system users. The farmer characteristics of education, innovativeness, and, most powerfully, age all predicted benefits obtained. However, benefits bore little relation to farm size. In terms of demographics, it seemed to be the younger farmers on the way up (who were better educated and innovative but less well to do at this point), not merely the larger farmers, who reported greater benefits. This suggests that benefit is not distributed equally but also that benefit does not accrue directly to the farmers because they are resource rich. Rather, benefit accrues to farmers who mobilize their resources to make effective use of the system.

Looking across the three levels of the information equity issue, we must conclude that inequity has been built into the system, because a particular market segment has been singled out for service. It may well be argued, just as the developers of FirstHand did, that market segmentation is necessary if a system is to be useful to someone. But, if society is to be segmented into markets, then society has an interest in making sure that all segments are served by their own system. Finally, we must conclude that there are inequities within the particular market segment served here. Even within the quite homogeneous group to which the system was offered and within the still more homogeneous group that used the system, demographic variables were still related to adoption, use, and benefit. However, other variables, such as information wants and needs, were correlated with the same outcomes. Thus, it can be argued that the particular combination of predictors of adoption, use, and benefit strikes far from the worst balance possible between the potentially conflicting goals of productivity and equity.

References

Carey, J. "Videotex: The Past as Prologue." *Journal of Communication,* 1982, *32* (2), 80-87.
Chen, T. C. "Computing Power to the People: A Conservative Ten-Year Projection." In R. J. Seidel and M. L. Rubin (Eds.), *Computers and Communication: Implications for Education.* New York: Academic Press, 1977.
Compaine, B. M. "Shifting Boundaries in the Information Marketplace." *Journal of Communication,* 1981, *31* (1), 132-142.
Dervin, B. "Communication Gaps and Inequities: Moving Toward a Reconceptualization." In B. Dervin and M. J. Voight (Eds.), *Progress in Communication Sciences.* Vol. 3. Norwood, N.J.: Ablex, 1980.
Dozier, D., and Ledingham, J. "Perceived Attributes of Interactive Cable Services Among Potential Adopters." Paper presented to the annual convention of the International Communication Association, Boston, 1982.
Dozier, D., and Rice, R. E. "Rival Theories of Electronic News Reading." In R. E. Rice and others, *The New Media: Uses and Impacts.* Beverly Hills, Calif.: Sage, forthcoming.
Ettema, J. S., and Kline, F. G. "Deficits, Differences, and Ceilings: Contingent Conditions for Understanding the Knowledge Gap." *Communication Research,* 1977, *4* (2), 179-202.
Katzman, N. "The Impact of Communication Technology: Promises and Prospects." *Journal of Communication,* 1974, *24* (4), 47-58.
Kline, F. G., and Clarke, P. "Communication Situations and New Technologies." In A. S. Edelstein, J. E. Bowes, and S. M. Harsel (Eds.), *Information Societies: Comparing the Japanese and American Experiences.* Seattle: International Communication Center, 1978.
Martin, J., and Norman, A. R. D. *The Computerized Society.* Englewood Cliffs, N.J.: Prentice-Hall, 1970.
Paisley, W. "Information and Work." In B. Dervin and M. J. Voight (Eds.), *Progress in Communication Sciences.* Vol. 2. Norwood, N.J.: Ablex, 1980.
Robinson, K. "Public Information and Electronic Publishing Services." *Journal of Communication,* 1982, *32* (2), 103-113.
Sigel, E. *The Future of Videotext.* White Plains, N.Y.: Knowledge Industry Publications, 1983.
Smith, A. *Goodbye Gutenberg.* New York: Oxford University Press, 1980.
Williams, R. *Television: Technology and Cultural Form.* New York: Schocken Books, 1975.

James S. Ettema is an associate professor of communication studies at Northwestern University. His research has focused on the social organization and impact of the media, including the new information technologies. He is coauthor (with Jerome Johnston) of Positive Images: Breaking Stereotypes with Children's Television *and coeditor (with D. C. Whitney) of* Individuals in Mass Media Organizations: Creativity and Constraint.

This study of teletext is as instructive about the pitfalls and rewards of field research as it is about the utility of the technology itself.

Teletext for Public Information: Laboratory and Field Studies

Martin Elton
John Carey

This chapter describes a program of laboratory and field research on broadcast teletext. In addition to presenting major results and summarizing their implications, it sets the program within the context defined by stakeholders in the teletext field. It also reviews the major methodological issues and practical eventualities that shaped the research.

The Teletext Medium

Teletext services provide users with a means of displaying "pages" or frames of text and graphic information on their television sets. In the usual form, frames are transmitted in a continuous cycle, using redundant space, the vertical blanking interval (VBI), in a

---

The research reported in this chapter was supported by the National Science Foundation under grant DAR 7824889. The authors wish to acknowledge the contributions of the project team. The authors alone, however, are responsible for the interpretations offered in this paper.

regular broadcast television channel. Less commonly, a whole television channel is dedicated to teletext, as it was in the experiment conducted in 1983 by Time, Inc., in San Diego, California, and Orlando, Florida.

Users display the frame they want by entering the frame's number into a keypad connected physically or ultrasonically to a special decoder attached to or built into the television set. The next time the frame is transmitted into the cycle, it is retrieved and displayed in place of the regular television programming on the channel. Some services allow teletext captions to be superimposed over regular programming on the screen so as to provide subtitles or news flashes.

Teletext has the virtues of simplicity, convenience and economy. The costs of decoders are low (approximately $150 in the United Kingdom), and production costs are insignificant compared to the costs of television. Development started in the United Kingdom during the early 1970s. Operational services followed a few years later, and by early 1984 penetration had reached 10 percent of television households. There are operational services today in Sweden, Austria, and Holland.

However, teletext is a decidely limited medium, especially when broadcast in the VBI. Each frame of information is the equivalent of approximately one and one-half column-inches of newsprint (between fifty and seventy words), normal capacity of a service is roughly a hundred frames. The fundamental relationship is that the time it takes to transmit a complete cycle increases with the number of frames; hence the time it takes for a requested frame to appear in the cycle also tends to increase. Typically, the average response time is six seconds or more.

Given the limitations of the medium (which make it appear very much a poor relation of its versatile cousin, videotex), some may wonder why it merits evaluation. There are good reasons. Teletext will prepare the general public for more sophisticated forms of electronic publishing and transactions. And, it has been demonstrated in Sweden that it is the medium of choice for subtitling for the deaf. It may enhance regular television programs, especially educational programs, by providing ancillary reference information. And, through advertising, it may provide an additional, albeit minor, source of revenue for commercial and public television stations. Some have suggested that teletext may also pose certain threats. It could attract television viewers during commercial breaks. It could divert classified advertising away from newspapers and magazines. It could compete for other uses of the vertical blanking interval.

Back in 1979, there was considerable activity in Europe. The

British and the French had established competing standards. The Canadian government was making a major investment in the development of another, more advanced standard. However, very little was happening in the United States. Fears were expressed that, if teletext was indeed socially valuable, American viewers would get it too late; the United States would not be a player in the international development of standards, and this could have an adverse impact on the balance of trade. Concern was also expressed that public television stations might be missing an opportunity to improve their ailing finances.

This situation was the background for a planning study undertaken in 1979 by the Alternate Media Center at New York University's Tisch School of the Arts on behalf of the Corporation for Public Broadcasting (CPB) and the National Telecommunications and Information Administration (NTIA). This study proposed to identify public policy issues and to make recommendations as to whether and how a field trial should take place.

Stakeholders for the Research

A variety of stakeholders were identified. The Federal Communications Commission (FCC) and NTIA would have a part to play in deciding the conditions under which teletext transmission would be allowed. Public broadcasting stations and CPB needed information on economics, viewership, and production issues so as to decide whether and how to introduce services. Commercial television stations and operators of cable television systems had similar interests. It was considered that teletext might become a particularly suitable medium for the dissemination of public service information from federal, state, and local government agencies as well as from community organizations. Clearly, the manufacturers of television sets had an interest, as did those associated with other, more established means of disseminating information—newspapers, publishers, and museums. In a field trial, there would be local stakeholders, too. The fact that most of the equipment used would have to be obtained from Britain, France, or Canada, each of which was advocating its own national standard in the U.S., added an unusual complication. The air was thick with competing technical and economic claims.

It was apparent that a good case could be made for a program of public funded user research that included a field trial as the primary component. It was objected, however, that if research on teletext was needed, it should (and sooner or later would) be conducted by the private sector. There were counterarguments that the results of proprietary research are released selectively to bolster the policy positions of vested interests; that proprietary research is not subject to the quality control of peer review; and that there are obvious economies of aggregation at a national level. In short, it was argued that public research would make a much more significant contribution to the informed debate from which policy should emerge. Eventually, a research program was funded by NSF and CPB, with additional support provided by NTIA and the U.S. Department of Health, Education, and Welfare. Its objectives were tied to the interests of the various stakeholders in ways described in the next section.

Issues in the Choice of a Research Plan

In developing a research plan for the teletext project, we were mindful of general issues associated with field trials, laboratory studies, and controlled field experiments involving new telecommunication technologies. Some of these issues are outlined in Shinn (1978); others are described in Lucas and Quick (1978) and Elton and Carey (1980). First, prototype equipment often does not work, or, if it does work, it may require frequent repair. This raises the question, Why not wait until the bugs are ironed out before conducting the social research? If one is concerned about influencing public policy or about guiding public service users, who may be confused by the competing claims of marketing groups, early research may be justified. However, a research team should be mindful of the costs associated with uncertain technologies, particularly in a field setting, as well as with problems in obtaining repair service and in keeping to a project timetable. These problems call for a flexible research plan and for the assignment of skilled personnel to the technical support system.

Another set of general issues concerns the decision to conduct research in a field setting. A laboratory setting offers greater cost economies and control of the research as well as a chance to examine clean issues that often become muddy in a real-world field setting. Conversely, a field setting provides an opportunity for the study of users' behavior under more, rather than less, natural conditions. It also offers a face validity that is important when research findings are directed to policy makers, and in many instances it offers greater visibility. This is positive if it leads policy makers to notice the research findings, but it can present a danger that they will attend to the wrong issues, for example, to a highly publicized but otherwise irrelevant single case. Associated with the selection of a field setting are the practical issues of managing a service, installing and maintaining equipment, maintaining liaison with local institutions, and other management tasks. Many researchers do not like such work or lack the training to accomplish it well. If a group lacks the skill or inclination to manage a field service, they must bring in and pay skilled managers.

A new telecommunication service presents yet another set of problems in a field setting: The service providers do not know at the beginning of the project how best to operate the service. Further, as they learn how to improve the service, the treatment will be changed, and the changes can confound the interpretation of findings. At the same time, an assessment of how a group develops skills in providing a new service is very important and can be helpful to others who may subsequently implement a similar service.

One alternative to the lab or field trials choice is a field experiment. It can offer the best or worst of both worlds. If the technology is very new and little is known about service provision, the danger signs are very bright. A field experiment is generally more costly than a field trial, since a field experiment brings with it additional requirements, such as control groups. If local publicity is likely, the methodological problems of control are likely to be much harder and more expensive to solve. Further, it is difficult to control treatments when equipment is unreliable and the service is undergoing rapid evolution. Equally important, it is hard to know what specific hypotheses should be tested during the earliest phases of a new service. One can formulate many useful research questions, but key hypotheses often do not emerge until later.

A concern about these and other general issues was complemented by several elements that were specific to our situation. First, there were very few teletext decoders that could be used with the U.S. television standard. With considerable difficulty, we were able to obtain sixty-four decoders. Further, we knew that reception problems associated with teletext would affect field testing in general and systematic sampling in particular. In reality, the problem proved to be far worse that we had envisioned, and, as we note later in this chapter, it had a strong impact on the sample of homes and public sites.

The teletext field trial would be costly. For that reason, we sought and received funding from four agencies, no one of which would have supported the entire effort alone. However, each agency had somewhat different expectations for the project. In particular, there was some conflict between the desire for scientifically rigorous research expressed by some agencies and the desire of others for a successful demonstration of the new technology. This conflict related not only to our funding sources but to many of the intended clients for the research findings, for example, federal agencies. In the planning study that preceded our formulation of the research design, we spoke to many federal agencies about their existing means of information dissemination and about the process by which they decided to create a pamphlet, produce a public service radio spot, or select another means for reaching the public with information. Many stated that they would require hard data about cost, reach acceptability, and social impact before deciding to use a teletext service as part of their information dissemination efforts. Yet, it was clear that their decisions about existing means of information dissemination had been made with little or no hard data about reach, acceptability, or effects. At the same time, they were quite aware of favorable press coverage generated by their media efforts or by those of other federal agencies. That is, visibility and publicity mattered to them.

The teletext project would involve working closely with public information providers, such as federal agencies, local libraries, and community service agencies. While many of these providers were enthusiastic about the project, they were experiencing budget cutbacks that affected their level of personnel support for the project. This meant that the burden of selecting, editing, and rewriting information for the teletext service would fall on our staff. At the same time, concern was expressed in the public broadcasting community that the project might turn the airways over to the federal government for information dissemination. While the project dealt primarily with consumer information from federal sources, critics felt that a dangerous precedent might be set that would allow a federal agency in the future to use teletext to propagandize.

In addition, the teletext project was to be housed within an institution, a major community-based public television station, that had little experience in the method of work required for teletext; that is, a teletext service is akin to a small newspaper or a radio news service. Further, while the station was enthusiastic about the project and had as an incentive the possibility that teletext might grow into a national service housed at the station, station personnel had little day-to-day incentive to change their ways of working. Institutional resistance to innovation under circumstances like these is well documented (Rogers, 1962).

The Research Plan

Our strategy for dealing with these general and specific issues must be described first in terms of our project plan and research design, then in terms of what actually happened. The research design and overall plan called for the project to be split into two distinct phases. The division represented an attempt to deal with funding problems (early discussions with funding agencies led us to believe that it would be impossible to fund the entire project in one stage), to get the technology under our belts before tackling large-scale field research, and to investigate general research issues in order to formulate specific hypotheses that could be tested in a second phase. Phase one had two components: a pilot trial and laboratory studies. Phase two was to include a larger field trial within which controlled field experiments were to be imbedded.

Pilot Field Trial in Homes and Public Places. The pilot field trial was designed to include forty homes and ten public sites. Our research instruments for the homes included a series of face-to-face interviews, diary records, kept by users, and meters attached to the teletext decoders that recorded each page request by time of day. The purpose of the public sites was to provide some visibility for the project, to increase the total number and the demographic spread of users, and to test the feasibility of a teletext information terminal at public locations. Our research instruments for the public sites included a meter that recorded each page request by time of day, a one-time written survey of user reactions, and nearly two hundred hours of systematic observation of user behavior at and near the teletext terminals. In addition, for a subset of the service, referral addresses and telephone numbers were specified in a unique form that enabled demands for further information generated by teletext to be identified.

Our use of ethnographic observation and notation techniques at the public sites, adapted from anthropological research, requires some explanation. Ethnographic notation can be viewed as a form of mapping, both of physical terrain and of social behavior. In this case, it included maps to scale of the public teletext sites that noted lighting, sources of extraneous sounds, entrances, pathways, and barriers, such as guard booths. Maps of traffic—that is, records, of those who used the terminal and those who passed nearby and had an opportunity to use it—were also included. The traffic records included time of day, site, and simple demographic characteristics of users and passersby. In addition, we recorded selected behaviors and entered a general diary description for each user observed. The observation sessions were conducted in three stages. During the first stage, which lasted approximately ten hours, behaviors were notated by a team leader who had training in ethnography. This phase was intended to uncover patterns that the field team could then systematically record in subsequent observation sessions. A second phase was employed to develop reliability among the coders. Field observations were conducted in the third and principal phase. The field observations attempted to balance notations by time of day, site, and codified behavior with opportunities and restrictions at individual sites. For example, during stage one, user responses to errors were identified as a potentially important issue (that is, if a person presses keys and does not receive the desired teletext frames, what does he or she do?). However, only two sites were suitable for the close, over-the-shoulder unobtrusive observation that was required in order to notate key-pressing behavior. We accepted this as a limitation and recorded such behavior at the two sites. In addition, each observer could freely note other behaviors besides those identified for systematic notation.

A number of issues were examined: who read instructions and when (most users did not read the instructions at all or read them only after trying to use the terminal and experiencing trouble); the phenomenon of staged approaches (many people approached the terminal in three stages, first stopping five to eight feet away, then moving to within three or four feet, and finally, walking up to the terminal); the shill phenomenon (many people are attracted to or feel more comfortable in approaching a public terminal that someone else is already using); and variations in use between those who are alone and those who are part of a group at the terminal. The public site research is described more fully in Carey and Siegeltuch (1982).

Laboratory Studies. The laboratory studies in phase one were intended to investigate a series of general issues that appeared to be both practically significant and suitable for testing in a laboratory setting (for example, how long will people wait for a frame of information to appear on the screen before irritation sets in?). Some of these issues had been identified prior to the start of our project. Others would be identified during the pilot field trial, which was to precede the laboratory studies. The laboratory studies had three goals: to provide findings independent from the pilot field trial research, to test issues or problems identified during the pilot field trial, and to help us formulate hypotheses that could be tested in phase two.

Expanded Field Trial. In phase two, the research design called for the field trial to continue and for the number of user homes to increase to approximately three hundred; the actual number was to depend on statistical findings at the pilot stage. Further, the homes were to be selected purposefully in order to support the project's research needs. A matched control group would be selected. While the bulk of the teletext frames was to offer a general information service, a portion would be set aside for use in the field experiments. These field experiments would test hypotheses developed in the latter part of phase one.

The use of multiple methods to gather data during phase one represented a straightforward methodological concern for matching appropriate measuring instruments with research questions under investigation. Further, it allowed the costs and value of each to be scrutinized. Some questions were redundant in case selected instruments failed (for example, if the meters did not work, we would at least have the diary records). In addition, we hoped for a synergy among the instruments—that is, by assessing behavior from more than one perspective, we hoped that it would be possible to learn something that single instruments, alone or additively, would not capture.

Implementation and Findings

Laboratory Experiments. Laboratory experiments focused on subjective reactions to frame design. Individual treatments corresponded to different ways of presenting the same information on a teletext frame (for example, by varying the use of color, framing, paragraphs, and bullets). Some designs used colorful graphics; others did not. The most important product of these experiments was methodological: A set of scales that could be reduced to three major factors accounted for about 60 percent of the variance in reactions to pages. The factors corresponded to attractiveness, clarity, and perceived usefulness of the information. Interestingly, as more features were added, attractiveness continued to increase, but clarity reached a peak and then fell off slightly.

One of these experiments was repeated using the same frame designs, but the evaluation took place in the homes of subjects involved in the field trial. Any differences from the results obtained earlier might have been due to the different population sampled, the effect of nine months of experience with teletext, or the residential, as opposed to the laboratory, setting. For frames that were primarily text, no significant differences were found. This increases our confidence in the stability of the scales. For frames containing artwork of various kinds, the results were less consistent, although statistical correlation with the earlier results was still significant. Other laboratory experiments focused on particular design issues; they are reported in Champness and de Alberdi (1982).

Field Trial. Engineering tests were conducted for several months prior to the start of the field service in order to identify geographical areas in which the teletext signal could be received. Teletext is much more vulnerable to reception problems than is regular television. Moreover, we were to be using an ultrahigh frequency (UHF) channel with above-average reception problems. Tests were conducted on our behalf by technical staff from the vendor of the teletext system that we had purchased, who used a Yagi antenna mounted on a van.

On the basis of these test results, we chose three neighborhoods as locations from which to select our sample viewers. Since the teletext service would be carried on the local public television station, we accepted the possible demographic bias involved in using its membership list as a sampling frame. Letters were sent to members inviting them to participate in the trial. We received just enough acceptances to select forty matched pairs of households, which provided us with a treatment and a control group.

Installation of the television sets incorporating teletext decoders started several months behind schedule. It was soon discovered that the tests of signal reception had been misleading. Reception was much more sensitive to location than had been assumed; the difference of a few yards could turn an adequate signal into an inadequate one. Moreover, an outside antenna was virtually essential. The results were further delay and expense, abandonment of the control group (which had to be raided for additional subjects), and the addition of some subjects from an apartment complex in a fourth geographical location. We did not regard the damage to the research design as serious, since this was the pilot phase. A control group had been incorporated primarily because it would be needed in the next phase, and we wished to estimate the procedural problems and costs involved in using it.

Although reception problems were resolved to a satisfactory extent, they continued to recur throughout the following year. Frequent site visits by a technician were required. Even so, a survey nine months into the trial showed that, at the time, about a quarter of the residential subjects were not receiving an adequate signal. Other technical difficulties required a correction to the technical design and retrofitting of all the receivers that had been installed.

Producing the Teletext Content. By intention, arrangements for producing the teletext service were complicated. At any time, more than a dozen different public and private organizations were contributing content in a variety of different forms. For example, the *Washington Post* composed pages on a terminal located in its own premises and transmitted them by telephone directly to computer memory at the transmission site. The National Weather Service used telex to provide information from which the central production team composed highly graphic weather forecast pages. Other organizations used mail or telephone to supply information from which teletext items were abstracted and pages were composed. Still others used facsimile transmission to send rough drafts of teletext pages to the production team.

This variety reflected two objectives. One was a desire to try different mixes of content and production techniques in order to find what worked well in the local situation. The other was to allow participating organizations to learn about teletext in a more direct way than would otherwise have been possible.

When the trial had been under way for six months, it became clear that our strategy would need to change. First, U.S. activity in the field of teletext had increased; several experimental and start-up services were in operation. Second, public research funds had become extremely tight. Third, evidence that the pilot field trial was even more seriously underfunded than we had thought was mounting: A second phase would cost considerably more for both production and research than we had originally anticipated. (Production of the pilot service accounted for about 70 percent of the roughly $1 million cost of the first phase.) Fourth, in all respects save one, we were making more progress in the research than we had expected. Consequently, we decided to extend the pilot by a few months, subject to funding, but not to proceed to a second phase. The funding for an extension of the pilot was forthcoming, and we proceeded accordingly.

Much had been learned about the use and attitudes toward teletext as well as about a range of production and methodological issues. The area in which progress was problematic was also the most ambitious, since it represented an attempt to assess the value of teletext in pursuit of specific goals related to information dissemination. For example, would public service information change attitudes, behavior, or both? Would people bring their children to a library event, have their blood pressure checked, or write for a public information brochure after learning about these opportunities from teletext? Interim findings suggested that our intended methods would work, but they would be difficult and expensive to apply. Even the simple matter of tracking usage of a service that was advertised on teletext was a major problem for agencies under severe financial pressue, and it posed a continuing management headache for the research team.

Service Format. During the trial, two alternative services were offered—a newspaper and a feature magazine. From June to December 1981, the teletext service resembled a small electronic newspaper. It emphasized timely hard information, such as national news and sports scores, which were supplemented by lists of community events and consumer price reports. From January to July 1982, the teletext service resembled a small electronic feature magazine. It emphasized graphics and stylized presentations of softer content, such as word games, children's stories, and electronic art.

The patterns of use for the two services were quite similar in the trial homes and at the public sites. The most frequently selected frames in the first service (the electronic newspaper) were concentrated among news, sports, weather, lists of entertainment events, and business information. Community information and consumer information frames were selected less often. Two very clear patterns ran through these content choices: Users frequently selected frames with timely information (for example, tomorrow's weather) and frames that were frequently updated (for example, news frames). It should also be noted that users tended to scan several information items briefly, rather than to read long items completely. For example, most users would read only the initial two or three frames of a ten-frame news story. The patterns of use for the second service, an electronic feature magazine, contained some surprises. Users continued to select timely information frames, such as local weather and a ski report, but they also responded well to electronic art, a chess puzzle, and charts of business trends. Indeed, a frame of electronic art was accessed more than any other during this period of use in the trial homes. (It ranked third in popularity at the public sites.) We believe that the art frame was very popular among children, who may have responded to it as a video game.

In comparing the two services, it appears that the small electronic newspaper had reasonably broad appeal, while the teletext feature magazine service was somewhat less popular among middle-aged males. Specific elements within each service were popular with specific segments of users. For example, games and electronic art appealed to teenagers, news was very popular among middle-aged users, and community information was attractive to blacks.

Teletext was used more frequently by males and by those under the age of forty-five. However, these patterns differed somewhat between the homes and the public sites. Use of teletext in the trial homes was slightly greater by males than by females. At the public sites, male users outnumbered female users by a ratio of four to one, although males and females passed near the terminals in about equal numbers. Other findings from research at the public sites suggest that teletext may have stronger appeal to those under forty-five years of age.

There was a strong novelty effect in the teletext homes, with early high levels of use dropping by more than 50 percent after two months. Once usage leveled off, the typical household watched the service three or four times a week, accessing approximately ten to fifteen frames at each session. Teletext viewing was more frequent between 8 and 9 A.M. and 5 and 7 P.M., with moderate usage throughout the rest of the evening. Approximately one third of the teletext sessions in the trial homes was not related to the watching of regular television programs, another third occurred just before or just after watching television, and the other third of the teletext sessions interrupted television program viewing. This pattern of viewing would appear to be favorable from a commercial broadcasting perspective; that is, users did not often switch from commercials to the teletext service, which was on public television. However, the design of the teletext keypad did not allow users to switch channels easily.

At the public sites, there was no evidence of a novelty effect. Variations in teletext use appear to have been related to seasonal shifts in traffic at a given site and to weather conditions. The number of users per day averaged twenty-six for all the sites. However, there was much variation — from more than fifty people per day at the Smithsonian Institution and a local community library to fewer than ten people per day at a senior citizen center and a journalism research library. Teletext viewing sessions at the public sites were generally short, averaging just over four minutes. In a typical session, a person viewed eight frames.

In general, residential users and survey respondents at the public sites indicated that they liked teletext. They were particularly favorable in their rating of the graphics and distinctly unfavorable about the speed with which frames appeared on the screen after the appropriate keys on the keypad had been pressed. Approximately 40 percent of respondents in the households and 50 percent of respondents at the public sites indicated that they would be willing to pay a premium, over the normal cost of a television set, to receive teletext in their homes. Willingness to pay was stronger among current heavy television viewers than it was among those who relied heavily on newspapers, magazines, and other forms of print for information.

Implications for Teletext Design

The field trial results as well as the laboratory studies have implications for service designers and system operators, notably public broadcasters. The design of a teletext service requires broadcasters to weigh the relative importance to viewers of the number of frames transmitted, the frequency of updating, and the sophistication of graphics. The significance of these variables derives from two relationships. One concerns production costs, and the other involves access time. For example, as the need to contain production costs increases, it becomes increasingly likely that sophisticated graphics or frequent updating will have to be sacrificed, since both activities are highly labor-intensive. Even when production costs are not restricted, a teletext designer must pay another cost for sophisticated graphics or a larger size data base — slower access time. Transmitting more frames or complex graphics enlarges the data stream. Since the data are transmitted in a continuous cycle, an enlarged data stream increased the waiting time for any given frame of information.

Thus, it is important to assess the importance that viewers attach to design variables. As noted earlier, users in the Washington trial expressed considerable dissatisfaction with the slowness of the service, even when the average access time was six or seven seconds. Our interpretation of the findings is that five to six seconds are the most that people will tolerate. Assessing the value of the number of frames in a teletext service, we found little evidence that the small size of the data base in the Washington trial made the service less attractive. Indeed, when the teletext service was reduced in size halfway through the trial, overall use both at the public sites and in homes changed very little. The frequency with which information is updated appears to have more importance for users than the size of the data base. Evidence from the residential sample suggests that the sections updated on a daily basis were used about three times as heavily as the sections updated once a week. While the graphics drew favorable comments from many users, it appears that they could have been curtailed somewhat without causing a serious loss of interest. Among residential users, for example, the two categories most heavily accessed during the first half of the trial were news and weather. The former was essentially text only, while the latter used the same graphics every day. This suggests that graphics become less important to users as they become accustomed to the service. However, graphics appear to have played an important role in attracting users to teletext.

Taken together, these findings suggest that people generally like teletext; further, many state a willingness to pay a modest one-time cost for the equipment that is needed to receive it. Once teletext is in homes, people are likely to use it for a short period (ten to fifteen minutes) every day or every other day. Service providers have a few options. They can appeal to a broad mass audience with brief news, weather, and sports information. They can devote all or part of the service to content areas that appeal to particular segments of the audience, such as consumer price information for middle- and lower-middle-income groups. In addition, the findings suggest that system operators may appeal to viewers more by spending production dollars on frequent updating of frames than by increasing the size of teletext service. Similarly, a modest level of graphics may render the service more attractive, but sophisticated graphics on every frame are likely to carry a high price in production costs and system access time.

In the short term, our research findings appear to be most useful to actual and potential members of the emerging teletext industry. At the time of the test, the climate was heavily influenced by extravagant speculation and misinformation. Concrete and extensive information, even from a single trial, can help to clear the air. Certainly, it was members of the industry, rather than the policy or academic research communities, who showed the most interest in the findings by their requests for technical reports.

It would be foolish to try to ascribe impacts to the results of the research program. They quickly became part of a much larger whole, which consisted of information emanating from other trial and operational services and information generated in continuing policy controversies.

The program clearly has implications for various stakeholder groups. For example, those who may be involved in operating a service should be warned by our technical difficulties and production costs, which were higher than anticipated. Since the costs are independent of the number of users, there is a strong argument for starting with national, rather than local, services. Technical and cost data would also have had implications for the adoption of technical standards for teletext, if the FCC had not decided to leave the problem of technical standards to be settled in the marketplace. There are implications, too, for those concerned with the design and market for teletext services.

Implications for Designing Field Trials. The program produced methodological results that can be expected to have value for other researchers.

Meters. While the meters were difficult to obtain and problematic to use, they provided indispensable data in the Washington trial. However, it is clear that the data would have been more valuable if additional funds had been spent on the meters. There are three requirements for the meters used in a research project, such as the Washington teletext trial. First, they should be robust. They should not be prone to accidental disconnection from the television set or from the electrical supply. Second, they should record viewing of regular television programming. Third, in situations where reception is bad, they should record each failed attempt to retrieve a page during a cycle.

Diaries. Self-completion diaries can complement meters in several ways, for example, by recording who used teletext. Although they are not a substitute for meters, self-completion diaries can also be helpful when meters cannot be used and when the data to be recorded are relatively brief and simple. However, two methodological problems should be noted. First, use of diaries increased the viewing of teletext during periods when users were asked to fill them out. There is reason to believe that such distortion diminishes (it did in the Washington trial) with successive diary completion periods. Depending on the measure used (for example, number of teletext sessions, number of frames accessed, amount of time spent using teletext, number of users active in a week) the inflation can lie between 20 percent and 40 percent.

The second problem in our experience with self-completion diaries involves underrecording. This problem is fairly well recognized in the field. In the Washington trial, the underrecording was systematic — that is, it produced a bias in the aggregate results. Index frames and secondary frames in a multiframe story were considerably less likely to be recorded. The use of a meter in our trial helped us to discover and measure both the diary errors and the influence of the diary recording process on actual usage. These findings suggest that another measuring instrument needs to be used to check self-completion diaries. First, it is useful to learn whether there is error or distortion in usage. Second, it helps to determine the direction of error or distortion and the degree of such error or distortion. In this context, it can be noted that the existing user research on teletext, which was conducted in Britain, had relied exclusively on diaries.

Finally, the novelty effect in the Washington trial should be noted. The trial homes required ten to twelve weeks before usage settled down. Unfortunately, many of the commercial trials involving electronic text have placed decoders in homes for a period of less than ten weeks. The results of those trials, which led to the investment of hundreds of millions of dollars by U.S. corporations as well as to a general marketplace conception about electronic text, can be called into question.

Lessons About Field Research. Most academic texts on research methods have relatively little to say about the practical realities of conducting research in a field setting except to discourage such research on the grounds that it is difficult to control the situation or to attribute an effect to a cause. However, unless one rules out field research categorically, it is important to ask, How should one plan a field project in which things go wrong, treatments change, and unanticipated research opportunities arise? The Washington trial provides a useful backdrop for discussions of these issues. Major elements in the original research plan either did not take place or had to be changed: There was no phase two, the laboratory studies in phase one came before and during the pilot field trial, rather than after it, as planned; and placement of decoders was dictated largely by reception patterns in the Washington, D.C., area. However, flexibility was built into the original plan and exercised in the field. For example, phase one research was designed to stand alone if necessary. The agenda of issues investigated in the laboratory studies was modified in response to the timing of this component in the research as well as to limitations in the technical system used to simulate teletext. Further, we accepted the restrictions on our opportunity sample of homes (the small number of decoders would not under any circumstances have permitted us to develop a sample that was representative of U.S. households) and looked to the public location terminals for information on how other groups reacted to teletext.

A few lessons can be drawn from these experiences. First, a field trial is not likely to proceed in line with the expectations of the research plan, so the researcher should be prepared for changes and for the unexpected. Second, the value of a carefully planned research design is not reduced by subsequent changes in the field. On the contrary, the planning process helps to strengthen a group's understanding of the object under investigation and of how to measure it. With such an understanding, it becomes possible to make informed adjustments in the research design. Third, it is often argued that social research is not like attempts to prove a mathematical theorem in that social variables are rarely pure or isolable from their environment. A field setting forces a social researcher to examine this argument. At the same time, the field setting encourages humility and demonstrates the necessity of stating explicitly the limitations of a given set of research findings.

Multiple Measures. The Washington trial also provides support for the use of multiple fixes on a problem or issue. For example, by using more than one measuring instrument, it may be possible to determine whether an instrument errs and, if it does, how much and in what direction it errs. The meters in the Washington trial served this function for the self-completion diaries. In addition, ethnographic research at the public teletext sites provided useful stand-alone data as well as a valuable complementary perspective on data from the written survey and from the meters at the public sites. It is unfortunate that some methodological texts dismiss observational research or damn it with faint praise. Yet, many of the observational recording techniques that anthropologists have developed are particularly appropriate in situations where researchers can make direct, face-to-face contact with users of new technologies. For example, we systematically noted the verbal statements of people approaching, using, and leaving the teletext terminal. An analysis of their spontaneous statements helped us to gain some understanding of their mental conceptions about the system (for example, many senior citizens, on discovering that a person had to press keys in order to use teletext, said, "Oh, it must be a new computer thing for the kids"). This form of observational recording, combined with detailed descriptions of selected behaviors, is also useful in discovering new issues or problems and in helping to formulate hypotheses for subsequent testing.

Laboratory Studies Versus Field Trials. Finally, the Washington trial throws some light on the appropriate uses for laboratory studies and field trials in the investigation of social applications for new telecommunication services. Key issues relating to effectiveness, design, or both can be formulated as hypotheses for controlled experiments in the laboratory. In addressing these issues, laboratory experiments are both powerful and relatively inexpensive.

Field trials are considerably more chancy and very much more expensive. However, they can address other important issues, such as who uses the service and to what extent. Moreover, generalization from laboratory experiments on a new service can be very risky, unless these is evidence to support the conceptual model of the service. Supporting or conflicting evidence can come from field trials. The relationship between field trials and laboratory experiments (and survey research) is clearly complementary. Laboratory experiments provide cost-effective means of testing a range of specific hypotheses, and they may help in designing a field trial. Field trials allow researchers to answer other questions, they make it possible to revise conceptual models and create new hypotheses, and they offer face validity. Given the open-ended nature of many field trials, the contributions of a variety of disciplines are potentially significant. Observational methods and unobtrusive measures are of particular importance.

References

Carey, J., and Siegeltuch, M. *Teletext Use in Public Places.* New York: Alternate Media Center, 1982.

Champness, B., and de Alberdi, M. *Measuring Subjective Reactions to Teletext Page Design.* Working Paper No. 2. New York: Alternate Media Center, 1982.

Elton, M., and Carey, J. *Implementing Interactive Telecommunications Services.* New York: Alternate Media Center, 1980.

Elton, M., and Irving, R. *The Value of Consumer Diaries in Studying Consumer Use of Teletext.* New York: Alternate Media Center, 1983.

Lucas, W., and Quick, S. "Serial Experimentation for the Management and Evaluation of Communication Systems." In M. Elton, W., Lucas, and D. Conrath (Eds.), *Evaluating New Telecommunications Systems.* New York: Plenum, 1978.

Rogers, E. *Diffusion of Innovations.* Glencoe, Ill.: Free Press, 1962.
Shinn, A. "The Utility of Social Experimentation in Policy Research." In. M. Elton, W. Lucas, and D. Conrath (Eds.), *Evaluating New Telecommunications Systems.* New York: Plenum, 1978.

Martin Elton and John Carey are members of the faculty in the Interactive Telecommunications Program, Tisch School of the Arts, New York University.

Our relatively limited experience with the use of microcomputers in education and the small number of educators with direct hands-on experience with the technology argue for the use of innovative research methods. Video case studies can serve a useful purpose.

Microcomputers in Schools: The Video Case Study as an Evaluation Tool

Henry T. Ingle

For more than seventy-five years, the use and effects of communication media and technology in education have been the object of systematic research inquiry worldwide (Grayson, 1982; Office of Technology Assessment, 1983). It is not surprising, therefore, that the introduction of microcomputers and related new information technology into the classroom should become an area of research inquiry and evaluation in the 1980s or that it should attract the attention of serious, long-standing media researchers as well as of individuals who have had little or no contact with educational technology and media research.

The fact that these new technological tools and their use in the classroom have become such a compelling topic for research inquiry will no doubt inject new vigor into the discipline of research and evaluation and at the same time stimulate new methodologies and approaches. This chapter reports on one such approach: the video case study as developed by Project BEST.

Funded by the U.S. Department of Education, Project BEST was a state technical assistance and capacity-building program. It

J. Johnston (Ed.). *Evaluating the New Information Technologies*. New Directions for Program Evaluation, no. 23. San Francisco: Jossey-Bass, September 1984.

43

relied on the use of audio and video teleconferences and an electronic mail network of microcomputers to facilitate state departments of education acquiring current knowledge and experience in the use of new information media, such as the microcomputer (Ingle, 1982, 1983). The acronym BEST stands for Basic Education Skills through Technology. The primary goal of the project was to enhance the capacity of state departments of education to work cooperatively with local education agencies in planning for and using new information technologies to improve the teaching and learning of basic skills. Working collaboratively with a number of professional education associations and forty-one states, the project produced a series of print and nonprint products, including four video case studies, based on the experiences of a sample of six districts in using microcomputers in the classroom.

Microcomputers: A Topic Appropriate for Video Case Studies

A number of recent research efforts has helped to describe the microcomputer revolution in schools. These efforts include several national surveys, such as those by Market Data Retrieval and Johns Hopkins University. Publications of the Center for Children and Technology at Bank Street College and the Office of Technology Assessment have provided much-needed research reports. These beginning efforts point to a number of interesting topics worthy of further inquiry and systematic analysis. These topics are indicative of the wide range of concerns that might be included in a research agenda on microcomputers in education during the 1980s. The Project BEST case studies identified a similar list. This convergence underscores the strengths of case study methods in instances when the identification of research issues is of paramount importance.

The video case study can also function as a powerful tool to clarify key issues for further study. Any one of the following concerns lends itself to further research scrutiny via the videotaping and case study methodology:
- developing insights about the effects of microcomputers in education, particularly at the elementary and secondary levels
- determining the extent to which educator criticism about the adequacy of instructional software, both in quantity and in quality, is valid
- specifying the types of in-service and preservice training activities that teachers and administrators need

- establishing criteria for the selection of microcomputer hardware and software by educational institutions
- answering equity concerns raised by differential access to microcomputers among girls and boys and among various minority and socioeconomic groups
- responding to claims of possible detrimental physical and health effects stemming from prolonged hours of microcomputer use
- exploring the growing belief among computer-using educators that children acquire increased higher-order reasoning and new cognitive information-processing skills as a result of systematic use of microcomputers for instruction
- redefining existing and emerging new roles among school practitioners in response to microcomputers
- undertaking systematic research on the development of software tied to particular teaching approaches and pedagogical requirements.

The video case study is not the only strategy for examining such issues, but it is an effective one. The array of practitioner experiences documented by our video case studies illustrates how the approach gets inside the issues. For example, they suggested that the renewed interest in educational technology stimulated by the appearance of microcomputers in the classroom is the result of several converging conditions: Microcomputers seem to be providing teachers, students, administrators, and parents with a refreshing, invigorating, and motivating source of energy and commitment to teaching and learning that has been missing from the school scene for a decade or more. National, state, and local governmental initiatives, coupled with private sector support, are making microcomputers and computer literacy a top priority in the promotion of educational excellence. Finally, educators who lack direct hands-on experience with microcomputers have a great need for information and knowledge that can assist them in making hardware purchasing decisions, understand the new technology, and know what kinds of uses are possible for their schools.

The video cases leave the reviewer with an understanding that microcomputers in the classroom, unlike educational innovations of the past, which were legislated from above, are largely a grass roots phenomenon stimulated by computer-using teacher enthusiasts, students who bring their own equipment from home, and parental pressure on school boards, administrators, and other teachers to make the technology part of the educational experience for a rapidly evolving information-age society. Thus, the case for microcomputers is hard to resist, and their rapid spread through schools since 1977 when they first became available has intensified the need for an information base that can sustain and guide planning decisions.

Although the field is too new to have generated a substantial research base, research-type efforts, such as the video case studies that will be described in this chapter, are helping schools to acquire the information needed to make informed decisions about the use of microcomputers in education.

Advantages of this Approach

Most of us are familiar with videotaping from years of observing on-the-scene news reporting on the nightly television news. Researchers and program evaluators in the behavioral, social, and medical sciences have for some years employed videotaping (particularly after portable, miniature recording equipment became available) for documentation, data collection, and analysis (Weick, 1968). Videotaping techniques have become useful for the documentation of phenomena open to alternative interpretations or for recording relatively new phenomena that are hard to observe firsthand or that have been observed by relatively few individuals under varying situations or in a few isolated instances. In this context, videotaping allows the researcher to make an audiovisual record of an observation, which he or she can then share with others and play repeatedly with the same fidelity as the initial observation. It can also be used to "manipulate time and space, to make minute examination of events, and to examine the action and behavior under review by several people after the fact" (Wilkinson and Brady, 1982). Videotape recordings represent a powerful tool for capturing and preserving an event in ways that no paper-and-pencil measures, paired human observers, prose, anecdotes, or audiotapes can document totally. Videotaping allows researchers to share actual data samples and make comparisons of conclusions as well as to edit and package the information to suit particular decision makers or particular requirements of information users.

When linked with a case study approach, as it was in Project BEST, videotaping offers a framework for the documentation and aggregation of disparate strands of qualitative and quantitative evidence that can provide answers to particular problem areas and help to develop assessment frameworks that can describe and appraise contemporary events and trends. The approach is particularly important for research and evaluation of microcomputer use, because rigorous research does not currently exist to help educators fully understand the use of new information technology in education. The knowledge is just in the process of being developed by reflective educators with early hands-on experience with the technology, and a decade or two may be required for it to be formalized so that it can be shared with others. These conditions reaffirm the role of the case study, coupled with on-site interviews and field observations, as a systematic research tool. It is not difficult to make a case for the approach at this point in the evolution of the educational applications of new information technologies, because there is more myth, rumor, and anecdotal information than solid research findings and sound premises for generating hypotheses and researchable questions.

The Project BEST Video Case Study Approach

As part of a U.S. Department of Education program to help determine national policies on technology and to help local and state school decision makers discover how they might use new technologies to support the basic skills instruction, Project BEST received nominations from around the country of school districts that had introduced microcomputers into classrooms and that had at least two years of working experience with them. Through telephone interviews and review of background documentation on the 125 nominees, six school districts were selected for in-depth site visits, classroom observations, and interviews by Project BEST staff. The resulting information was brought together in four videotapes that aggregated the experiences of individual schools in order to make generalizations about the issues that schools faced in working with microcomputers in the classroom. *Getting Started with Technology* discussed why educators were turning to technology and how they became interested in it. *Learning and Teaching About the Technology* showed how staff and students learn to use and become comfortable with the microcomputer as a tool. *Hardware and Software Selection* examined considerations in the selection process and the procedures and evaluation criteria used. Finally, *Teaching with the Technology* showed classroom applications of the technology in instruction and management. Each of these thirty-minute videotapes presents the aggregated experiences of personnel in the six school districts that Project BEST staff visited. Key ingredients of each videotape, then, are clips selected from the videotaped examples recorded in each site.

The districts visited were Albany, Ohio; Ann Arbor, Michigan; Cincinnati, Ohio; Cupertino, California; Fairfax County, Virginia; and Plains, Montana. These were not necessarily lighthouse districts.

Rather, in their size, wealth, geographic location, urbanicity, and experience with computers, they reflected the diversity of school districts in this country. They offered examples of what could be done that other districts in similar situations might emulate.

To supplement the videotapes, a companion print profile on each of the school districts was prepared. The tapes and print profiles are not case studies in the traditional sense, because they make no effort to tell the complete story. Instead, they provide snapshots of the districts' status in fall 1982 and winter 1983 regarding applications of computers, particularly microcomputers, to the improvement of basic skills instruction, classroom management, and school administration. The profiles follow the sequence of the videotapes. Each profile contains six sections: A district summary provides a capsule overview of the school district. A section on history discusses why the district became interested in microcomputers, how they were introduced, and milestones in the early planning effort. Another section describes how school staffs were prepared to use microcomputers and how students learned about the machines. The fourth section reviews the brands purchased and the criteria used in selection, procedures followed to evaluate software, and types of software used. A section on applications describes ways in which computers were being used to support classroom instruction and management. A spring 1983 update summarized what had happened since the original site visit and videotaping. Finally, each school district profile contains the name and address of an individual who can be contacted for further information and a list of printed information about the district's microcomputer plans and programs.

Strategy for Developing Video

Development of the Project BEST video information modules was a cooperative process involving a design team composed of researchers and video production specialists. A coordinator assigned to each module had ultimate responsibility for the focus and content of all its elements. Personnel from the design team conducted the research for the modules and prepared the written materials. Video production staff from the Maryland Instructional Television Center were responsible for videotaping. Standardized interview and observational forms were developed for use in the field.

The research process involved seven principal steps. In step one, individual telephone interviews with key school staff in each district documented how schools addressed the four topics of the modules: the getting-started process, how staff and students learned to use and become comfortable with the microcomputer as a tool, considerations followed in selecting hardware and software, and classroom applications of the new technology in instruction and management. In step two, the design team conducted an initial site visit to each district in order to see firsthand what the telephone interviews had described and to conduct preliminary on-site interviews with key personalities. In step three, the design team returned to each district to conduct more in-depth interviews to cull information from support documents, to make systematic classroom observations, and to videotape the process.

Collectively, steps one, two, and three provided a reliability check on the information being collected. Reliability is often a source of difficulty and potential bias for case study methods. Through use of a common set of twelve key questions asked of all individuals contacted, conflicting responses could be identified and, where appropriate, resolved by cross-checking and investigative questioning techniques designed to document key aspects that consistently surfaced in interviews, group discussions, and on-site observational activities. The decisions on what to tape were based on the results of this search for congruence and reliability.

Step four began the process of synthesizing the information across sites in order to produce the four video information tapes. Members of the design team brainstormed on the process observed, and raw footage from the videotapes made at school sites was screened. The audio portion of each tape was transcribed, and the information provided by tapes and transcripts was categorized and indexed according to problems, issues, and concerns being analyzed. Controversy surrounding not the factual documentation of reality but the esthetics of documentation can often surface at this stage of the work. Consequently, criteria for the final selection of video materials need to be discussed by the group. Video production crews and research staff can conflict on this score. In Project BEST, researchers and video producers had a friendly tug of war about what to include and exclude. The video crews tended to prefer attractive pictures and images that met their own technical and esthetic criteria, even if these preferences misrepresented the research findings. In Project BEST, the researcher and video producer reached a compromise involving voice narrations over an array of visually appealing materials. This solution allowed interesting visual material to be used without compromising the research protocols and findings. Researchers need to bear the possibility of such conflict in mind when working with video and film production crews who have no training in research methods. In the long run, it may be better to train researchers to use videotaping technology than it is to turn video production personnel into researchers.

In step five, scripts for the initial video modules were drafted from materials on the particular issue, problem, or concern being addressed in the module for each school site. In step six, responses were aggregated, and evidence was marshalled to form some generalizations about the particular problem or concern being addressed. In step seven, tapes depicting these conclusions were prepared, reviewed by the project design team, reedited as needed, and packaged with print support materials for dissemination to participating Project BEST state teams.

Summary and Conclusions

The video case study approach used by Project BEST illustrates the advantages of this methodology for the study of new information technology in education. The approach appears to have had three advantages. First, it provided an aggregate of vivid, real-life instances and concrete, everyday examples of how school practitioners were actually handling the concerns raised by the introduction and use of microcomputers. These examples provided a basis for alternative interpretations and generalizations that could easily be communicated to and understood by others. Consequently, the results helped those who viewed the videotapes and read the profiles to understand the microcomputer phenomenon in education and to make decisions appropriate to the circumstances of their particular school.

Second, the video case study approach allowed the research team and others who viewed the resulting materials to compare the salient issues in classroom microcomputer applications across several school sites. The process generated a consistent set of generalizations that were applicable to educational practice in a number of school settings. As a result, existing assumptions and stereotypes could be explored, discussed, and in some instances debunked and discarded. In the process, a research agenda of areas appropriate for further inquiry evolved. This agenda was matched with research and evaluation methods that could focus effectively on the specific nature of the problem or issue at stake.

Third, the video case study approach provided those who viewed Project BEST videotapes and reviewed print profiles with contextual information and frameworks for interpretation that normal research reports and professional articles did not.

The experiences of Project BEST underscore the value of the video case study as a research strategy which is still in its infancy and which needs further use to test its applicability to other phases of research and evaluation inquiry. The videotaping approach is valuable not only for data-collection functions but also for analysis and interpretation as well as for the discussion of findings and results in an entertaining and forthright manner. (The Project BEST video and print case studies are available for a nominal charge from the Association for Educational Communications and Technology (AECT) in Washington, D.C. For further information contact AECT, 1126 Sixteenth Street, N.W., Washington, D.C. 20036 (202) 466-3361.)

References

Grayson, L. P. "New Technologies in Education." In H. E. Mitzel, *Encyclopedia of Educational Research.* (5th ed.) New York: Free Press, 1982.

Ingle, H. T. "Linking the New Information Technologies to the Work of State Education Agencies: A Profile on Project BEST." *Maryland Journal of Higher Education,* 1982, *6,* 7-16.

Ingle, H. T. "Project BEST: What Is It? Who's Involved? And How Are States Benefiting?" *AEDS Monitor,* March-April 1983, 31-34.

Office of Technology Assessment, United States Congress. *Information Technology and Its Impact on American Education.* Washington, D.C.: U.S. Government Printing Office, 1983.

Weick, K. E. "Systematic Observational Methods." In G. Lindzey and E. Aronson (Eds.), *The Handbook of Social Psychology.* Reading, Mass.: Addison-Wesley, 1968.

Wilkinson, L. C., and Brady, M. *Videotaping in Classrooms: A Guide for Researchers.* Program Report 83-1. Madison: Wisconsin Center for Education Research, University of Wisconsin, 1982.

Henry T. Ingle is dean of the School of Communications at California State University, Chico. From 1981 to 1983, he served as Director of Project BEST for the U.S. Department of Education and the Association for Educational Communications and Technology.

The diffusion and the characteristics of new communication media provide evaluation research with opportunities and challenges.

Evaluating New Media Systems

Ronald E. Rice

This sourcebook is neither the first nor the most visible sign that new information technologies (*new media* hereafter) are rapidly diffusing throughout our society to homes, organizations, communities, and institutions. However, it is indicative of a growing awareness that evaluation research needs to consider new media both as valuable and appropriate contexts for analysis and as an opportunity to apply expertise and insights to an increasingly significant component of social activity. This chapter has two parts. The first reviews the process by which new media are diffused. The second describes some characteristics of new media that have implications for evaluation research.

New Media: Increasingly Pervasive but Underevaluated

The term *new media* includes a wide variety of communication technologies, such as interactive cable, videodisc, electronic mail and computer conferencing, videotex and teletext, personal computers, communication satellites, cellular radio, information retrieval systems, office information systems like word processing, and knowledge worker support tools connected by local area networks. As with other communication media, these systems include capabilities for the creation, transmission, storage, and reception of communication content—

J. Johnston (Ed.). *Evaluating the New Information Technologies.* New Directions for Program Evaluation, no. 23. San Francisco: Jossey-Bass, September 1984.

whether it be textual (words or numbers), graphic, or audio. However, the new media have some characteristics in which they differ substantially from radio, newspapers, books, television, and telephone. These differences are due to the fact that the new media are facilitated by computers, sometimes by microprocessors embedded in the medium itself, sometimes by direct use of a mainframe, sometimes by a computer-managed network. As a result, the new media add processing of content to media functions and increase the interactivity that users or communicators can experience. In the next section of this chapter, these and other characteristics of the new media are considered in detail.

Some figures show that the new media are becoming increasingly pervasive. Knowledge Industry Publications (1983) reports that the percent of total consumer media spending on home computers, video games, cable and pay TV, and videocassette recorders rose from 7.5 percent in 1978 to 30.8 percent in 1982. By 1987, this increase is expected to grow by 411 percent for home computers, 104 percent for videocassette recorders, and 85 percent for cable and pay TV. Between one and three million microcomputers were sold in 1982; this figure is expected to rise to between seven and ten million by 1990. Already, five percent of U.S. homes have a microcomputer, and around 20 percent of its companies do (Blundell, 1983; "Personal Computers in the Eighties," 1983; "The Computer Moves In," 1983). Using a probability sample of 2,209 elementary schools, Becker (1983) reports that 42 percent of schools had one or more microcomputers that were used for instruction purposes, while fewer than 10 percent had five or more; the figures for high school were 77 percent and 40 percent, respectively. Videogames in arcades generated $7 billion in 1982, greater than the revenues of the movie and record industries combined. Besides the almost 8,000 public arcades, there were 14,000,000 home videogames, representing around 10 percent penetration ("National Family Opinion," 1983; Nielsen, 1982; "Video Games Go Crunch," 1983).

There are at least eighty pilot or commercial public videotex systems operating around the world. This figure does not include teletext systems or in-house closed-user groups. The Dow Jones News Retrieval system boasts more than 70,000 subscribers, while the more residentially oriented services, such as CompuServe and The Source, each have around 40,000 subscribers (Rice and Associates, 1984). Public data base providers experienced a 30 percent increase in customers in 1982; six of the largest providers served more than 20,000 users each. More than 700 providers offer more than 1,500 data bases (Russell, 1983).

More than seventy commercial electronic messaging systems were available in 1983. These systems comprised nearly 400,000 formal accounts (mailboxes), while corporate systems involved around 225,000 mailboxes, and The Source, CompuServe, and microcomputer networks supported 77,000 mailboxes (Burstyn, 1983; Panko, 1984; Sandler, 1983). In the office, about 35,000,000 workstations are expected to be in place by 1990. More than 40,000 word processing units will be delivered in 1984 (International Data Corporation, 1983). The *Wall Street Journal* has reported that nearly 85 percent of the Fortune 500 companies planned to install teleconferencing facilities; the number of installed teleconferencing rooms is expected to rise from 575 in 1981 to nearly 4,000 in 1986 as part of a 61 percent growth rate in teleconferencing use (Quantum Science Corporation, 1981).

These sample figures demonstrate the increasing presence of these technologies. These media can be seen as so new that their validity as research topics is still in doubt. Alternatively, this newness can generate inappropriate and atheoretic research. But, both of these extreme responses disappear when the term *new* is seen as relative. It must be seen in that light because all communication media have been seen as new when they were introduced.

By taking the perspective that recent media are new relative only to the past, it becomes both possible and useful to apply theories and evaluation approaches developed and tested in studies of earlier media. For example, summative and formative evaluations of prosocial and instructional television have provided analytical tools and research results that are now being used in the early evaluations of educational computing by children at home and in school (Johnston and Ettema, 1982; Palmer, 1981; Williams and others, 1981; Rice and Associates, 1984). Or, theories and evaluations of news reading can be applied to videotex system design and use. But, in both cases, the differences created by the facilities of the new media require research to pay attention to different variables, different policies, and different potentialities: In particular, evaluators still have some opportunities to affect system design and implementation, which was not often the case with the mass media. Thus, the newness of recent communication technologies should not blind us to the context of prior communication and evaluation research, but it should also signal new challenges and new opportunities.

When we examine the published literature on new media, it becomes clear that this opportunity is still largely untapped. An analysis of four on line bibliographical data bases (Sociological Abstracts, Social Science Citation Index, Magazine Index, and Management Contents) available through the DIALOG data base service revealed considerable interest in the new media in the business, trade, and popular literature but almost no interest in the new media within the scientific community (Rice and Associates, 1984). From 1974 to 1982, 1.12 percent of all articles in the Management Contents file could be retrieved using keywords related to the new media; percentages for the Magazine Index, Social Science Citation Index, and Sociological Abstracts were 0.5 percent, 0.1 percent, and 0.09 percent, respectively. Further, a year-by-year analysis showed a nearly exponential growth in the percentage of business articles mentioning the new media, a noticeably increasing growth after 1977 in the magazine data base, and a decline in the sociological data base (the social science citation data base cannot be broken out by year). The ERIC data base, which contains education-related materials, including many unpublished conference papers and technical reports, showed a steady rise in materials on instructional television between 1966 and 1970, a plateau lasting six years, then a continuing decline. The number of materials on computer-assisted instruction showed a similar pattern through 1977, but then it began to grow, and it has continued to grow ever since. Finally, a content analysis of conference papers presented at annual International Communication Association meetings indicated increasing coverage of new media, with 3 percent coverage in 1973 and almost 10 percent in 1983.

The implication of this cursory review of the literature is that the scientific community, except for isolated pockets, such as educational computing and communication conference papers, has not considered the new media as worthy of attention, but the business, trade, and popular communities have. Evaluation researchers can take advantage of this attention gap by considering projects that have a component involving new media and by reporting their research in sympathetic journals; the business and popular community will find interest in such efforts. It may be especially productive to develop joint projects between communication researchers and program evaluators that can take advantage of their mutual skills and interest in analyzing the new media and their social contexts. However, evaluation efforts need to adapt data collection, research designs, and analytical approaches to the characteristics of the new media. Those characteristics are discussed in the next section.

Characteristics of New Media: Implications for Evaluation

Newness. Although extreme responses to the newness of recent communication technologies should be avoided, it is nonetheless true that these media offer new communication functions, introduce new technological designs, require new human capabilities, and suggest new specifications of contemporary theories. Therefore, it is entirely appropriate and necessary for evaluations of new media to consist of or to include case studies. Critics of this approach argue that the results, which are rich in process and contingency analysis, cannot be generalized to other instances of new media use. In reply, it can be said that we have as yet little understanding of the process by which individuals and organizations adopt, use, and respond to communication systems, so that work needs to be done to establish the range of possibilities, identify problems with variable definition and data collection, develop standards for later comparison, and develop theory that can be tested in subsequent replications.

For example, in a study of the adoption of word processing by 200 organizations, case studies of a subset of the companies revealed four distinct ways of managing such installations. Each approach involves an increasing level of communication among operators, supervisors, and authors, with concomitant increases in flexibility, creativity, and integration in word processing use (Rice and Associates, 1984). The insights provided by open-ended interviews and construction of the adoption process have significant implications for improving efficiency, effectiveness, and employee satisfaction. Yet, they could not have been postulated before the research was conducted, and, indeed, they could not have been deduced from responses on the 200 organization-level questionnaires. This four-system model of word processing innovation can be tested and refined, it can inform the general diffusion of innovations model, and it can be used as a general framework for evaluations of the implementation and management of future office information systems.

Case studies also have much to contribute in the way of developing baseline data on use and impact. There are considerable archival and historical survey data about the mass media with which contemporary use of the media can be compared, but there are no such resources for the evaluation of new media. Thus, while a cross sectional survey of multiple organizations will reveal aggregate relationships, a case study conducted over time can reveal typical trends that would otherwise confound cross sectional relationships. It seems, for instance, that use of computer-mediated communication systems typically rises to an early peak, then declines to some lower plateau (Rice, 1982; Rice and Paisley, 1982). Knowledge of such trends can be used to time the data collection in other evaluations to guide subcategory analysis, and, when not supported, to generate alternative explanations for system usage. For example, an evaluation of a university electronic mail system showed a decline in reported system usage only among the highest users; the overall equilibrium in system usage was posited as an attitudinal rather than a behavioral condition. That is, the interaction of individual media preferences, task attributes, organizational roles, and media characteristics constituted a media style that intervened between access and use, thereby effectively disassociating perceived benefits of electronic messaging from actual use of the technology. The consequence was that a straightforward evaluation showed a high correlation between system use and reported benefits. However, the media style analyses showed that perceived benefits were unevenly distributed and could not be guaranteed for each organizational member simply by making the technology available (Rice and Case, 1983).

As already mentioned, the newness of the new media does not deny—in fact, it illuminates—the utility of theory and research on more traditional media. Thus, new media research needs to seek out relevant models and theories. For example, a common initial response to text-oriented new media (personal computers, electronic messaging and computer conferencing, videotex, office information systems) is that they will depersonalize human relationships because they cannot transmit nonverbal and affective cues. This interpretation is a rather straightforward application of the combination of technological constraints in transmission band width with an understanding of the different kinds of human communication coding. However, a framework for cross-media comparisons has been developed that specifies this very broad technical analysis. Called the *social presence* model of media use, it has been described most thoroughly by Short and others (1976). These authors argue that, due in part to technical constraints, different media transmit different amounts of social presence, that is, different perceptions of the presence of users of the medium. Levels of social presence are typically indicated by respondents' evaluation of media on such scales as unsociable–sociable, insensitive–sensitive, cold–warm, and impersonal–personal. Perceptions of the sociability and appropriateness of different media do not depend strictly on technical constraints but also on preexisting attitudes, familiarity, and preferences. For example, replications of social presence analyses typically order common media by declining level of social presence in this manner: face-to-face, television, multispeaker audio, telephone audio, and business letter. However, the other component of the model described by Short and others (1976), the task context, is equally crucial. Some tasks are more technical, objective, and formal; other tasks are more social and emotional in nature. For example, consider two official organizational tasks: a routine request for updated information and a strategic negotiation between two executives. These very different contexts affect the appropriateness of any given medium. In the electronic messaging study cited earlier, this new medium was rated as appropriate for the following tasks by the percentages of managers: exchanging information (100 percent), asking questions (95 percent), staying in touch (84 percent), exchanging opinions (81 percent), generating ideas (73 percent), decision making (47 percent), exchanging confidential information (30 percent), resolving disagreements (15 percent), and bargaining and negotiating (18 percent). Similar rankings are found for computer conferencing systems (Hiltz and Turoff, 1978; Rice and Associates, 1984). Thus, the social presence literature is a useful framework for comparing new media (Johansen, 1977).

However, because the new media are new, they have yet to achieve stable perceptions in beginning users, and they are flexible enough to be used in different ways over time. Thus, experience and context of use may well be contingent conditions for evaluating the appropriateness of new media. For example, experienced computer personnel using the same electronic messaging system were more likely to rate the system as appropriate for generating ideas, decision making, resolving disagreements, and bargaining and negotiating than managers were (Rice and Case, 1983). Experienced computer conferencing users were more likely to rate the medium as appropriate for the more socioemotional tasks (Hiltz and Turnoff, 1981; Rice and Associates, 1984). So, as the medium becomes less new, users' attitudes toward the new media are likely to change, depending on task, organizational role, and media preferences. Therefore, from an organization's perspective, the impacts, benefits, and applications will also evolve. Evaluation has a role in identifying these changes and in facilitating desirable evolution.

Communication Processing. It is essential to view new media as processors of communication. It is true that many applications of the mass media and of some of the new media consist essentially of information delivery or transmission. However, as already noted, the digital signaling and computer processing involved in new media expand the range and nature of communicative activities. Consider computer conferencing. Because the conferencing program can be designed to create specific communication structures (such as equal access and participation by all, sequential polling, centralized decision making, hierarchical access priorities, and so forth), the evaluator needs to know the goals, constraints, and philosophy of the system's communication structure before he or she can interpret the actual usage patterns and user responses. Conversely, precisely because individuals in a computer conference that has been designed to equalize participation do tend to participate more equally than participants in face-to-face groups do, there is less likelihood of a leader emerging, less likelihood of consensus about the final group decision, and more likelihood that it will take some time to reach a decision (Kerr and Hiltz, 1982; Rice and Associates, 1984). Further, difficulty in reaching consensus does not seem to be related to the quality of the group's decision; indeed, the minority that holds out for its decision in a computer conference, which in a face-to-face group may have succumbed to nonverbal and interpersonal peer pressure, occasionally holds on to a superior or more creative decision. Evaluation needs to consider trade-offs that are consequences of the medium before assessing the utility of the system.

Because communication involves interactions and exchanges among individuals, the level of analysis can be seen as one of relation or interaction, not of a single individual's use or a group's aggregate usage. That is, attention to the communication process involving new media leads research to consider communication networks. A network is a pattern of relations (Rice and Richards, 1984; Rogers and Kincaid, 1981). Network analytic methods have been used by sociologists interested in social structure, anthropologists interested in community and kinship structure, health service agency evaluators interested in client and agency relationships, and managerial researchers interested in organizational structure. However, rigorous network analysis requires censuses, not samples, of users and research budgets and organizational patience impose constraints. Nevertheless, the emphasis on near-censuses may be salutary. Otherwise, system evaluators may lose sight of an important characteristic of new media: A communication system becomes more important as more people have access to and use it. There are two methodological implications for communication system evaluators. The first is that results from a study in which only a small number of the possible users in a given social system actually use the medium are likely to be misleading, because the full benefits of the system cannot have been realized; the users have been communicating only among themselves, and they still use other channels to communicate with nonusers. The second is that network analytic techniques, which reveal clusters and patterning of interactions, the most central and most isolated communicators, and where information flows in the system, seem to provide fruitful approaches for evaluations of new media (Rice, 1982). However, these techniques require more complete data and sometimes more sophisticaed statistical expertise than the techniques used to evaluate traditional mass media.

Availability of Computer-Monitored Data. Computers in

various forms are fundamental to new media, and computers can collect data about system use. Typically, such data come from studies of information retrieval systems and of computer-mediated communication systems. Data analysis can focus on the frequency, type, and context of errors; the timing and duration of use; specific commands or sequences of commands; use of categories of messages (such as private-public, single-multiple, messaging-conferencing); interaction patterns among senders and receivers; textual content for semantic, linguistic, interaction, or topical interest; and traditional system evaluation of hardware and software performance (Chandler, 1982; Danowski, 1982; Hamilton and Chervany, 1981; Hiemstra, 1982; Penniman and Dominick, 1980; Rice and Borgman, 1983).

There are several advantages to such data. The computer can collect them automatically, and it can administer, prompt, and manipulate controlled experiments (Hiltz and others, 1982). Data collection can remain unobtrusive, reducing such threats to validity as demand characteristics and interviewer bias (Webb and others, 1981). Further, the data are not based on remembered or perceived reports of communication behavior; instead, they represent actual communication behavior. Discrepancies between the two kinds of data are often quite considerable (Bernard and others, 1982; Rice and Associates, 1984). It is nearly as easy to capture the entire census of user behavior with the computer as it is to sample, which satisfies the need to measure the relations among all users. Systems can monitor usage over their lifetime (or at least over the lifetime of the evaluation), so longitudinal evaluations of complete populations of users are possible. Thus, the process of adoption and use as reflected in communication behavior can be described and analyzed to an extent impossible without computer-monitored data. For example, Rice (1982) used monitor data for ten research groups (each comprising about fifty people) who used a nationwide computer conferencing system for twenty-five months. There were 87,000 interactions in the data set, which revealed network patterns within and across groups and how they developed over time; at the same time, the data set tested a model of interaction posited on electronic, not face-to-face, communication. Heeter and others (1983) analyzed Nielsen meter data about cable television viewing and channel switching that involved selected portions of millions of transactions. Such uses of computer-monitored data not only can reveal processes that cross sectional and survey data cannot, but they also foster replications and reevaluations, because they avoid the measurement and reliability problems created by questionnaire wording, sampling error, and response inaccuracy.

However, the ability to capture and use such data has certain disadvantages. The massiveness of the resulting data sets creates budget problems, because the programming of the monitoring functions requires support from systems staff, and it may also require extensive preprocessing of the data tapes. Processing and management require extensive time commitments. Moreover, the expertise needed to accomplish all the necessary processing is not readily available. There are also the questions of privacy, confidentiality, and the ethics of collecting data on people's communication behavior. Usually, certain portions of the data will be available to evaluators as part of a pilot or government-funded project. Others solutions to privacy concerns include consent statements, randomized identification numbers, bypassing of content, and aggregate reporting. The allure of reliable behavioral data may obscure the fundamental question about the meaning of such behavioral data. While attitudes may be based on false perceptions, attitudes are what subjects report and what they reveal to others. The discrepancy between reported behavior and actual behavior does not necessarily imply that actual behavior at one time influences behavior and attitudes at a later time as much as it does that attitudes affect behavior the first time. Thus, evaluators must identify how the different kinds of data can be useful before they retool to analyze computer-monitored data. The fundamental hurdle, however, may lie in integrating the evaluation component early enough to request the capture of these data in efficient and usable form.

Media as Systems. The awareness that mass media are embedded in social context and that they are part of economic, political, and technological systems clearly must be extended to new media. Looking at media in terms of organizational, institutional, and environmental contexts has received constant, if not primary, attention in communication research (Hirsch, 1977; Rice and Associates, 1984). Within organizations, the introduction of automatic processing systems and information systems has spurred the development of a sociotechnical perspective, which bases the design of work and understanding of the impacts of telecommunications on a view of the work group as an interaction among attributes of the technology, social needs of the group, and characteristics of the work task (Bostrom and Heinen, 1977a, 1977b; Cummings, 1978). Further, media themselves—particularly new media, because of the integration of different telecommunication technologies, including computer facilities—necessarily involve a diverse array of designers, vendors, adopters, users, and evaluators. Thus, evaluations of new media need to consider the systemic context of the media and to identify system elements that are sufficiently relevant and consequential to include. One framework for identifying these components is a four-dimensional matrix consisting of stakeholders, criteria, domain, and method.

Stakeholders are system actors who have an interest in the system (or, more narrowly, in the outcome of a specific evaluation). Bryk (1983) examines stakeholder-based evaluation. Considering the interests and perspectives of various stakeholders increases cooperation, deepens understanding of the system or program, and raises the salience of evaluation results. Moreover, the chance of significant errors in system design and implementation increases when alternative perspectives are not considered in the evaluation (Hamilton and Chervany, 1981; Kling, 1980). This is because information systems are systems: Many actors are involved, and many people are affected, but the linkages between these groups are often not clear to participants. Evaluation has a role to play in uncovering the assumptions, effects, and relevance of various stakeholders. At least six categories of stakeholders are involved in new media systems: macrosupport—funders—of development and evaluation for governmental or policy purposes; regulators, as of telecommunications and legal matters; social and cultural activists, including critics and proponents of new media in such contexts as children's use of videogames or invasion of privacy by computerized record keeping; industry representatives and system designers, who are concerned about such matters as technical standards in videotex systems, system performance, cost-efficiency evaluations, and the proprietary nature of evaluation results; administrators—personnel managers concerned about access to use and support, support staff concerned about development priorities and user requests, or work group leaders who desire simple but flexible design; and users, whether potential (the "computer illiterate," persons in low-income communities where there are no personal computers in schools), organizations and institutions (libraries and legal firms will have very different needs for and tolerances of on line data bases), groups (who may value group cohesion over decision-making efficiency), user networks (which may have lower tolerance for unreliable value-added networks because there is no other means for communicating with most network members), and individuals (who may be concerned about employment impacts, ergonomics, and ease of use). The stakeholder approach is not necessarily economical or easy to manage, because it requires extensive evaluator commitment and interaction with the interested parties. And, the interaction itself can bias the interpretation of analyses.

The criteria or goals of an evaluation are influenced not only by stakeholders but also by the training, theoretical orientation, and mandate of the evaluators. Criteria for success or failure may include resource distribution, system functionality, political processes (whether related to public concerns or to organizational politics), knowledge creation and dissemination, cost (amount, relation to benefits, source of funding), social benefits (such as quality of life), demands on users' skills (with implications for training, career advancement, and system rejection), and social structure (who gains and who loses access to communication and information).

Another dimension of the evaluation matrix consists of the domain of analysis or the level of communication behavior. Specifying the domain causes different networks of communication and different uses of the media to become salient. These domains range from institutions and society to groups, dyads, and individuals. These domains then interact with stakeholders and criteria in identifying the attributes and impacts of new media that should be measured and evaluated. For example, in assessing the relationships between office automation and organizational productivity, most organizations have used very traditional and narrow criteria for productivity when calculating the benefits of systems. Word processing may be cost-justified on the basis of reduced keystrokes or increased paper throughput, but this approach ignores the multiple levels of criteria for performance that coexist (perhaps uneasily) in an organization. The mission of the organization, such as increased short-term profits for stockholders, may mandate very different measurements of benefits than organizational purpose (a strategic target for accomplishment of mission) would. Mission would emphasize the return on investment of an inventory control system, while purpose might emphasize reduced customer turnover because of improved service. Such organizational functions as planning and purchasing may emphasize customizing of system language, even though this might reduce cross-function communication. Further down the hierarchy of organizational performance, processes represent the form, not the content, of organizational behavior. For example, managerial style in one organization might emphasize face-to-face communication over telephone or memo communication; clearly, an electronic messaging system will be used less in such an organization, but it also requires a lower criteria of use to be considered successful. The activities—that is, the observable behaviors that make up each process—involve the different kinds of tasks discussed in my comments on social presence. Different activities can be assessed for their contribution to the organization's mission, purpose, and function. So, an evaluation effort might wish to consider how well meetings and computer conferences satisfy given criteria, rather than to assess the new medium by itself. Finally, the sequential stages involved in performing the activities constitute actions. Productivity evaluations can measure the amount of time and resources used to make a successful telephone call to transform the same message content across various forms (phone message, notepad, message note, formal calendar, dictated response, official letter).

The methods dimension of the evaluation matrix includes the full range of analytical tools now available to evaluators. As already mentioned, it includes network analysis as well as considered use of computer-monitored data. Because of the new and evolving nature of the new media, their increasing integration with other media and with other work units and processes throughout the organization, and the complex contingent nature of media effects, it is also necessary to take advantage of new analytical perspectives that focus on change. Statistically, this involves the use of Markov analysis, pooled cross sectional time series, LISREL, overtime and multidimensional scaling, and case studies (Hannan and Young, 1977; Hewes, 1978; Monge, 1982; Woelfel and Fink, 1980).

Another approach specifically addresses the changing perceptions as nonusers become new users, then experienced users. If new media do indeed change the ways in which people work and communicate, then attitudes and perceptions should change as well. Thus, three kinds of change are possible. The first kind of change, alpha change, is change in level on a particular scale: Users do more work, or they are more satisfied. The second kind of change, beta change, involves the extension of a prior scale: After the introduction of word processing, operators have higher expectations for turnaround and text flexibility, so earlier evaluations of work done by typing may have to be adjusted downward in retrospect. The third kind of change, gamma change, involves a shift in the dimension used to evaluate work: Integrated office systems allow users to be more effective and change their work processes, criteria very different from efficiency of typing (Rice and Associates, 1984). As Tapscott (1982, p. 20) concluded from an evaluation of an office automation system, "the findings suggest that as access to information improved, so did expectations regarding what is possible and perceived requirements regarding what is necessary." The methods used for measuring and identifying these kinds of change are well introduced by Terborg and others (1980).

To summarize, evaluation approaches must match new media systems in their complexity and evolution. Such matching requires attention to different levels of and interactions among the four dimensions of the evaluation matrix proposed here.

Early Adoption Stages and Innovative Adopters. At this time, the majority of new media implementations are pilot systems, funded demonstration projects, installations in selected organizational departments, or acquisitions by innovative individuals. This set of characteristics has crucial implications for evaluation.

One implication is that the only population that users of new media represent is new users. Thus, it is difficult for consumers of evaluation (say, managers or agency funders) to know how the results should affect policy. The managers who used the electronic messaging system that Rice and Case (1983) evaluated were chosen to be social role models for other university managers, so that diffusion would be facilitated. At the same time, both perceived benefits and usage patterns are likely to be quite different for later users. The farmers selected as users in the agricultural information system demonstration sponsored by the Department of Agriculture (Rice and Paisley, 1982) were stratified by farm size (an indicator of gross revenues) to control for economic differences in explanations of videotex use. None of the demographic variables was successful in predicting reported or system-monitored use, but the farmers' innovativeness (measured by the number of other farm innovations previously adopted), coupled with a functional interest in weather information, was associated with system-monitored use. Thus, even when there are evaluation opportunities to improve inference strengths, new users still can be discriminated by their general innovativeness. Other traits associated with innovativeness are likely to be confounded with reported effects of and attitudes about new media.

Further, because the new media are complex systems, they are often tested in real organizational or social settings. Thus, it is very difficult to locate a control group with which comparisons can be made. Moreover, separating subjects into users and nonusers limits the potential positive benefits of the system, because everyone does not interact. Even if early users in a pilot system are relatively representative (or even if enough variables are measured to enable postproject statistical controls to be performed), rival hypotheses cannot easily be rejected through analyses of behavior and attitudes in similar groups of nonusers. Some approaches to this problem are possible, however: Tapscott (1982) reports an office automation study that involved a control group; users can be studied over time (both before and after implementation) to take into account within-group historical trends, and early users can be compared with more experienced users. Although cross-system evaluations are difficult to conduct, they are necessary if the rival hypothesis of system-specific results is to be rejected. Only Kerr and Hiltz (1982) have reported such multisystem analyses.

Because both the new media and their diffusion through social and organization contexts are in early stages, formative evaluation has a greater role to play than it does in traditional media evaluations; early or interim results can be used in later system refinements and management actions, particularly because the integration of the computer with the medium makes continuing development of applications possible. Thus, some portion of evaluation efforts can be directed at identifying ways of managing and applying technology to improve the likelihood of desired benefits later in the implementation process. For example, in the word processing study mentioned earlier, a summative evaluation of the organizations at the less creative sites might have concluded that they had implemented the innovation successfully although they were mired in a narrow and limiting form of adoption. Rather, a model of innovation that posits reinvention (the adaptation of an innovation after its initial adoption) will look not at whether organizations adopt or do not adopt but at systematic conditions in the organization that foster reinvention (Rice and Rogers, 1981). In this case, precisely because information about information systems is needed if we are to understand the technology and the potential for wide-ranging applications, organizations that supported operator-supervisor-author communication experienced greater benefits from the technology.

Simultaneity of Influence. One consequence of many of the characteristics of new media just described is that evaluation efforts must reject simple notions of one-way causality. Because media systems exist in social systems, because they are complex, because they are new, because they involve communication and networks of users, it is difficult to posit first causes. Indeed, consequences reverberate throughout such systems. An organization that fosters reinvention in simpler media will experience changes in work design that will motivate the adoption of more sophisticated office information systems (Giuliano, 1982; Strassman, 1980). Individuals may report attitudes toward and perceived benefits from new media, but those perceptions may have been the motivations for system use in the first place (Kerr and Hiltz, 1982; Lippitt and others, 1980; Rice and Case, 1983).

Thus, we need to consider the role and the acceptance of new media in a complex information environment. For example, the longitudinal analysis of computer conferencing users mentioned earlier explicitly avoided a deterministic analytical approach; rather, it assumed a probablistic communication process and tested not impacts but different models of how social systems would develop over time and what attributes of information flow would be significant components of the networks' patterns over time (Rice, 1982). Theoreticians of computing impacts argue persuasively that computing is a web or package that changes, develops, constrains, and is constrained (Kling, 1980). One implication for analysis is that the effects of media on other media become valid foci of evaluation. For example, what are the consequences for local newspapers when electronic publishing (such as videotex) becomes an economic reality? Will access to computing at home and at school improve literacy in general and book reading in particular? Electronic messaging in organizations tends to reduce the use of memos and telephones but not of face-to-face communication, yet managerial time is the most expensive and apparently most oriented to face-to-face interaction. What trade-offs among media are possible and beneficial? Low-power television, and direct broadcast satellites will all compete for some of the same advertising and consumer spending resources that once was the sole preserve of television, which in turn had encroached on radio and newspapers resources. What design and marketing strategies will facilitate success of these new transmission media?

Summary

Several authors have been credited with the indictment that, on the train to progress, we all have seats facing backward. Researchers still have an opportunity to turn around and see where we may be going. If we cannot see far ahead, we may at least be able to describe what is just ahead or what we are passing by so that we can assist those who are deciding which tickets to purchase. In this chapter, I have indicated some of the ways in which evaluation research can take note of characteristics of new media that will inform analysis, enrich interpretation, and enliven implications.

The growing use of new media evidenced by market penetration figures and industry projections is as yet unmatched by scholarly attention, references retrievable from major on line data bases indicate. The attention gap that such comparisons reveal is not necessary, as there is considerable precedent in past evaluations of mass and educational media. Indeed, existing research approaches and theoretical foundations can be applied to the study of new media. However, new media exhibit characteristics that require alterations in traditional evaluation efforts. These characteristics include, but are not limited to, newness; processing of communication content and flows; availability of computer-monitored data; the systemic nature of media, which requires a multidimensional evaluation effort; early adoption stages and innovative adopters; and simultaneity of influences. The resultant systemic interaction of new media within and with their environments requires new evaluation perspectives and methodological approaches. But, it also presents evaluation with opportunities to cross disciplinary and stakeholder boundaries, to inform and unite what may otherwise be disjointed and opposed actors and components of new media systems.

References

Becker, H. J. "How Schools Use Microcomputers: Reports from a National Survey." Baltimore: Center for Social Organization of Schools, Johns Hopkins University, 1983.

Bernard, H., Killworth, P., and Sailer, L. "Informant Accuracy in Social Network Data V." *Social Science Research,* 1982, *11,* 30-66.

Blundell, G. "Personal Computers in the Eighties." *Byte,* 1983, *8* (1), 166-182.

Bostrom, R., and Heinen, J. "MIS Problems and Failures: A Sociotechnical Perspective, Part 1: The Causes." *MIS Quarterly,* 1977a, *1* (3), 17-32.

Bostrom, R., and Heinen, J. "MIS Problems and Failures: A Sociotechnical Perspective, Part 2: The Application of Sociotechnical Theory." *MIS Quarterly,* 1977b, *1* (4), 11-28.

Bryk, A. S. (Ed.). *Stakeholder-Based Evaluations.* New Directions for Program Evaluation, no. 17. San Francisco: Jossey-Bass, 1983.

Burstyn, H. "Electronic Mail: Evolving from Intracompany to Intercompany." In A. Smith (Ed.), *AFIPS Conference Proceedings: 1983 National Computer Conference.* Arlington, Va.: AFIPS Press, 1983.

Chandler, J. "A Multiple Criteria Approach for Evaluating Information Systems." *MIS Quarterly,* 1982, *6* (1), 61-74.

"The Computer Moves In." *Time,* January 3, 1983, pp. 14-24.

Cummings, T. "Self-Regulating Work Groups: A Sociotechnical Synthesis." *Academy of Management Review,* 1978, *3* (3), 625-634.

Danowski, J. "Computer-Mediated Communication: A Network Analysis Using a CBBS Conference." In M. Burgoon, (Ed.), *Communication Yearbook 6.* Beverly Hills, Calif.: Sage, 1982.

Giuliano, V. "The Mechanization of Office Work." *Scientific American,* 1982, *247* (3), 148-165.

Hamilton, S., and Chervany, N. "Evaluating Information Systems Effectiveness, Part 1: Comparing Evaluation Approaches." *MIS Quarterly,* 1981, *5* (3), 55-70.

Hannan, M., and Young, A. "Estimation in Panel Models: Results of Pooling Cross Sections and Time Series." In D. R. Heise (Ed.), *Sociological Methodology 1977.* San Francisco: Jossey-Bass, 1977.

Heeter, C., D'Alessio, D., Greenberg, B., and McVoy, D. "Cable Viewing." Presented at the annual meeting of the International Communication Association, Dallas, 1983.

Hewes, D. "Process Models for Sequential Cross Sectional Survey Data." *Communication Research,* 1978, *5,* 455-482.

Hiemstra, G. "Teleconferencing, Concern for Face, and Organizational Culture." In M. Burgoon, (Ed.), *Communication Yearbook 6.* Beverly Hills, Calif.: Sage, 1982.

Hiltz, S. R., and Turoff, M. *The Network Nation: Human Communication via Computer.* Reading, Mass.: Addison-Wesley, 1978.

Hiltz, S. R., and Turoff, M. "The Evolution of User Behavior in a Computerized Conferencing System." *Communications of the ACM,* 1981, *24* (11), 739-751.

Hiltz, S. R., Turoff, M., Johnson, K., and Aronovitch, C. "Using a Computerized Conferencing System as a Laboratory Tool." *SIGSOC Bulletin,* 1982 (4), 5-9.

Hirsch, P. "Occupational, Organizational, and Institutional Models in Mass Media

Research." In P. Hirsch, P. Miller, and F. Kline (Eds.), *Strategies for Communication Research.* Beverly Hills, Calif.: Sage, 1977.

International Data Corporation. *1983 Information Processing Industry Briefing Session.* Framingham, Mass.: International Data Corporation, 1983.

Johansen, R. "Social Evaluations of Teleconferencing." *Telecommunications Policy,* 1977, *1* (5), 395–419.

Johnston, J., and Ettema, J. *Positive Images: Breaking Stereotypes with Children's Television.* Beverly Hills, Calif.: Sage, 1982.

Kerr, E., and Hiltz, S. R. *Computer-Mediated Communication Systems.* New York: Academic Press, 1982.

Kling, R. "Social Analyses of Computing: Theoretical Perspectives in Recent Empirical Research." *Computing Surveys,* 1980, *12* (1), 61–110.

Knowledge Industry Publications. News Release, February 25, 1983. White Plains, New York: Knowledge Industry Publications, 1983.

Lippitt, M., Miller, J., and Halamaj, J. "Patterns of Use and Correlates of Adoption of an Electronic Mail System." In *American Decision Sciences Proceedings,* Las Vegas, 1983, *1,* 195–197.

Monge, P. "Systems Theory and Research in the Study of Organizational Communication: The Correspondence Problem." *Human Communication Research,* 1982, *3,* 245–261.

"National Family Opinion/New Electronic Media Science Study Reveals Hidden Structure in the Home/Computer Hardware Market." *Media Science Newsletter,* January 1983, pp. 1–15.

Nielsen, A. C. "The Outlook for Electronic Forms of Message Delivery." *Nielsen Newscast,* 1982.

Palmer, E. "Shaping Persuasive Messages with Formative Research." In R. Rice and W. Paisley (Eds.), *Mass Communication Campaigns.* Beverly Hills, Calif.: Sage, 1981.

Panko, R. "Electronic Mail." In K. Tackle-Quinn (Ed.), *Advances in Office Automation.* New York: Wiley, 1984.

Penniman, W., and Dominick, W. "Monitoring and Evaluation of On Line Information System Usage." *Information Processing and Management,* 1980, *116,* 17–35.

"Personal Computers in the Eighties." *Byte,* 1983, *8* (1), 171–182.

Quantum Science Corporation. *Report on Teleconferencing Market.* New York: Quantum Science Corporation, 1981.

Rice, R. E. "Communication Networking in Computer Conferencing Systems: A Longitudinal Study of Group Roles and System Structure." In M. Burgoon (Ed.), *Communication Yearbook 6.* Beverly Hills, Calif.: Sage, 1982.

Rice, R. E., and Associates. *The New Media: Communication, Research, and Technology.* Beverly Hills, Calif.: Sage, 1984.

Rice, R. E., and Borgman, C. "The Use of Computer-Monitored Data in Information Science and Communication Research." *Journal of the American Society for Information Science,* 1983, *34,* 247–256.

Rice, R., and Case, D. "Computer-Based Messaging in the University: A Description of Use and Utility." *Journal of Communication,* 1983, *33* (1), 131–152.

Rice, R. E., and Paisley, W. "The Green Thumb Videotext Experiment: Evaluation and Policy Implications." *Telecommunications Policy,* 1982, *6* (3), 223–236.

Rice, R. E., and Richards, W. "An Overview of Network Analysis Methods." In B. Dervin and M. Voigt (Eds.), *Progress in Communication Sciences.* Vol. 6. Norwood, N.J.: Ablex, 1984.

Rice, R. E., and Rogers, E. M. "Reinvention in the Innovation Process." *Knowledge: Creation, Diffusion, Utilization,* 1981, *1* (4), 499–514.

Rogers, E. M., and Kincaid, L. *Communication Networks: A New Paradigm for Research.* New York: Free Press, 1981.

Russell, J. "All the Info, All the Time—On Line." *Data Management,* 1983, *21* (2), 41-42.
Sandler, C. "Electronic Mail: The Paperless Revolution." *PC: The Independent Guide to IBM Personal Computers,* 1983, *1* (9), 52-58.
Short, J., Williams, E., and Christie, B. *The Social Psychology of Telecommunications.* New York: Wiley, 1976.
Strassman, P. "Office of the Future." *Technology Review,* 1980, *82* (3), 54-65.
Tapscott, D. *Office Automation: A User-Driven Method.* New York: Plenum, 1982.
Terborg, J., Howard, G., and Maxwell, S. "Evaluating Planned Organizational Change: A Method for Assessing Alpha, Beta, and Gamma Change." *Academy of Management Review,* 1980, *5* (1), 109-121.
"Video Games Go Crunch." *Time,* October 17, 1983, p. 64-65.
Webb, E., Campbell, D., Schwartz, R., Sechrest, L., and Grove, J. *Nonreactive Research in the Social Sciences.* Palo Alto, Calif.: Houghton-Mifflin, 1981.
Williams, F., LaRose, R., and Frost, F. *Children, Television, and Sex-Role Stereotyping.* New York: Praeger, 1981.
Woelfel, J., and Fink, E. *The Measurement of Communication Processes.* New York: Academic Press, 1980.

Ronald E. Rice is an assistant professor in the Annenberg School of Communications at the University of Southern California. He has completed several studies of such new media as computer conferences and electronic message systems. For the communication research field, he sees the new media as having as much potential as newspapers and television for the expansion of communication theory.

Characteristics of the new information technologies have implications for both summative and formative evaluation. The instability of most technologies, coupled with their novelty for most users, calls into question the value of experimental summative studies, and the interactive character of many instructional technologies challenges the traditional formative paradigm. Case studies and field experiments can help to cope with this situation.

Research Methods for Evaluating the New Information Technologies

Jerome Johnston

In the last few years, new information technologies have proliferated at a rapid rate. With the aid of the microprocessor, many of the older technologies have acquired new potential, while brand new devices have appeared that have no precedent at all. The stand-alone microcomputer promises to bring new efficiencies to the work of schools and businesses. In many sectors of our society, people are exchanging information, both text and numbers, over great distances; electronic message systems and computer conferences have become quite popular. Teletext gives television new potential. Stations can now broadcast supplementary text and graphic information that teletext subscribers can decode. Videotex offers more versatility; users can summon up customized information from a data base or initiate purchases and banking transactions from home or office. With the help of a laser beam, immense quantities of pictorial and textual information can be packed on a videodisc. When coupled with a microprocessor, that information can be retrieved in random patterns to suit the needs of a variety of users—especially students trying to learn new skills. The capacity to retrieve only the information that a learner needs to know represents a great advance for educational technology.

Evaluation activities have played a part in this revolution in several ways. Needs assessment data have been used to decide what new products should be developed. Formative research has been used to help shape products to meet the needs of the users for which they are intended, and, to a limited extent, impact studies have assessed how the new technologies have changed the settings or people who used them. But, the contribution of evaluation has not been as large as it might have been, for several reasons. Product development has been in the hands of people who are unfamiliar with the contribution that formative research can make. In the last fifteen years, formative evaluation has become a highly refined strategy for the development of educational products, such as instructional television (Crane, 1980). It assumed this role because many of the products were developed by a small group of production houses that recognized the value of the contribution that evaluators joining forces with television producers and content specialists could make. The developers of the new information technologies do not come from this tradition, and they are not familiar with the contribution of formative evaluation to product development (Kerns, 1983). Summative evaluations of the new technologies have been scarce for several reasons. First, there has not been a demand for evaluation data. Historically, such demand occurs when controversy has arisen over a particular intervention. It was just such controversy over the Head Start program that led to the growth of educational evaluation in the late 1960s. Few vocal critics have questioned the value of implementing the new technologies. Second, the new technologies emerged at a time when the traditional funders of such research—the National Science Foundation and the National Institute of Education—were hard-pressed to support such activity. Third, evaluators have found it difficult to adapt traditional evaluation strategies to the fast-evolving new technologies. This chapter explores the characteristics of these new technologies and the contexts in which they are being used, and it makes recommendations about appropriate evaluation strategies.

The Audiences for Technology Evaluation

What is evaluation? For our purposes here, evaluation can be described as the use of social science research methods to gather information that can help one or more audiences or stakeholders decide what next steps to take or how to value steps that have already been taken. Stakeholders are people who have an interest or stake in the outcome of such research. In Ettema's research on videotex, described in Chapter One, three stakeholders were identified: the manufacturer of the hardware, the financial institution that wanted to test the technology as a new service, and society in general. Evaluation is designed to provide impartial information of a scientific character that allows decision makers to act rationally as they decide on future courses of action. In recent years, a number of audiences has desired evaluative data on technology. The first group can be called technology's entrepreneurs. Its members are the many hardware and software companies responsible for creating the products that are proliferating around us. This group has two information needs. The first is information about the general demands of market segments for new technologies. The new technologies have great potential, and they can be transformed into new products with relatively little retooling. While traditional market research has helped many companies to modify their product line so that it better meets the locus of consumer demand, it has not been able to deal with the larger question. For what basic information needs will a new product be attractive enough to yield sales? The entrepreneurs are in great need of better ways of tracking these kinds of consumer needs. The second type of information that this group needs is formative information about how to package or configure new products. This information includes knowledge about appropriate ergonomics of hardware, attractive packaging, and specific functionalities required to meet users' needs.

The second audience for evaluative data on technology is the broad range of potential consumers for the new technologies. Here, we see a variety of information needs. The first is for simple exposition regarding new products. The novel character of many new technologies leads potential consumers to raise questions as simple as What does it do? In the school market, school officials perceive a continuing demand from various segments of the community to incorporate computers into the school curriculum. Yet, many administrators have little idea about what could be gained from putting computers into classrooms. How would classrooms be different if microcomputers were present? How many microcomputers would be necessary for whatever they might do? What might children learn if microcomputers and appropriate software were available? How much training would teachers and students require? How much maintenance would be required? These and other questions plague decision makers for whom the technology seems not to solve identified problems but to be thrust upon them. Consumers who have decided to secure a technology need product ratings. This need is perhaps the most obvious in the home and school market for new technologies. Individual consumers need consumer reports to help them acquire hardware and software. In the industrial sector, consultants will bring their expertise for a fee to any manager who is disposed to install a technology in his or her organization. The third type of information needed involves costs and benefits. Consumers need information about the increased efficiency or accuracy that new technology can bring. Such information is very hard to come by. The difficulty stems from the fact that many of the technologies are not simple replacement technologies—not an electric typewriter instead of a manual typewriter; rather, they fulfill a number of different functions.

The third audience for evaluative data on technology is society at large. Here, the questions are related to whether the new technologies represent social benefits. Who will benefit from a large-scale move to a new technology? Will certain groups be disenfranchised if information is distributed by an electronic means instead of by print? If microcomputers are indeed an important educational tool, are they available only to wealthy homes and schools, or are they distributed among all segments of society? Such questions as these are only now emerging, because the technologies are so new that they have yet to become part of the fabric of society.

Attributes of the New Technologies

A number of characteristics of the technological revolution are worth noting, because they affect how one looks at the role that research can play in their creation and evaluation.

Moving Target. To state the obvious, all the new technologies represent moving targets. Innovations that today astound our sense of the possible can become outdated in a very short time. Research takes time and deliberation. Evaluators may be pushed to their limit when trying to deliver information on today's product before attention moves to a new product. In program evaluation, change in the nature of what's being evaluated has always presented a challenge. The utility of evaluation is related to its ability to provide feedback to those who must make judgments about future directions. If evaluators are to aim at utility, then evaluation must adopt speedier methods.

Novelty. The most common form of evaluation collects reactions from users or from groups affected by a device or program. Most potential users are unfamiliar with the new technologies. A paradigm that depends on user reactions to new products must question the meaning of responses when they are based on hypothetical situations. This requirement leads many evaluators to propose studying groups that use prototypes of a new technology. While this approach is useful, there are some compromises in using early adopters, especially if the early adopters are self-selected. Their responses are subject to change as personal experience or use by others in their social network increases.

Interdependencies. Complex interdependencies are implicit in most of the new technologies, both in the process by which new products are developed and in the implementation of the new products in the intended settings. Such products as videodisc with instructional components require design teams composed of instructional designers, programmers, human factors experts, and television producers. The notion of instructional design teams is not a new concept. It was pioneered at Children's Television Workshop for the creation of "Sesame Street" and "Electric Company." However, we now see a new cast of characters on the design teams, and many have not worked together before. Complex interdependencies can also be seen in the implementation of new products. For example, new computerization procedures have eliminated one personnel function at AT&T. In the past, supervisors received a listing of repair orders and assigned work to repair people. In the new automated system, repair personnel get their assignments directly from a computer terminal (Bush, 1983).

Many management information systems are designed to facilitate the flow of information among the many departments of an organization. To make such flow possible, data from many parts of the organization are assembled in a central computer. For example, a single management system can involve coordinating the data bases of marketing, finance, and manufacturing to allow high-level managers to make decisions about new production. In the past, each division of the company collected information on its own operations, summarized that information in terms that those outside the division could understand, and then distributed it throughout the organization in a series of face-to-face meetings. Data were frequently assembled in ways unique to divisions, and the human interface provided the common language that allowed decisions to be made. Under centralized computer systems, data must have uniform specifications to allow consistency in data retrieval and presentations. Purchasing, payroll, and accounts receivable are often asked to change long-standing procedures in order to accommodate the system's requirements. Implementing a computer-based management system in an organization requires a great deal of coordination among all departments.

Nonlinearity of Educational Programs. Educational research has a long tradition of assessing the impact of educational programs, and there is an extensive literature on the impact of instructional television, textbooks, and even complete courses that use multiple ingredients, such as lecture and textbook. Most of this research assumes that all students are presented with essentially the same materials. In viewing an educational film, students may perceive it differentially or remember material selectively, but all students are presented with the same material. In contrast, most of the new computer-based educational products are branching. That is, each user accesses instructional material according to diagnostic branching points at which he or she responds to test questions. Thus, a single videodisc with a microcomputer program to drive it can be described not as a single educational product but as multiple educational products, each of which varies with the needs of students.

Self-Monitoring. By virtue of the microprocessors built into most of the new technologies, the machines themselves are capable of collecting data on the amount and type of use by those who use them. This capacity has presented a host of problems as well as new potential for understanding the phenomenon under study. On the positive side, it makes it possible to collect data on how users interact with the machine — how long a session lasts, what functions are called, and what sequences are followed. From these data, many things can be inferred about the utility and comprehensibility of hardware or software functionality. Moreover, microprocessors make it possible to present functions to users in a predetermined order or to present material in an order that corresponds to some experimental manipulation aimed at testing different approaches. Finally, questionnaires that once were administered by paper and pencil can now be administered electronically while respondents are logged onto the computer. On the negative side, keystroke data are, by definition, voluminous. The mere management and reduction of such data into useful indexes is a time-consuming and costly process. Ettema (Chapter One) reports using the entire computer budget of his videotex research project simply to manage and analyze the data collected by the machines themselves. The question of validity is equally problematic. How shall the data points be interpreted? Consider a computer-based educational program. If a frame of information is accessed quite frequently but for a very short duration of time, is it because the frame is very useful or is it because poor directions in a preceding frame cause it to be accessed by accident? Rice and Borgman (1983) report that machine measures of usage correlate only about 0.38 with self-report data on usage of the same function.

Evaluation Strategies

The literature on educational evaluation makes a useful distinction between formative and summative evaluation. The term *formative evaluation* was coined by Michael Scriven to encompass the type of evaluative activities that are used to help shape a new educational product.

They include small-scale rapid-turnaround assessments of audience reactions to format, plot, storylines, and other features of the delivery device or the content. The focus is typically on pieces of the complete product, and the questions focus on appeal and comprehensibility. The term *summative evaluation* refers to evaluation of the use or impact of a completed product. Using large samples of either gatekeepers (for example, teachers or parents) or the target audience (for example, students), such research focuses on the adoption, utilization, or impact of an entire product, such as a television series. The distinction between formative and summative evaluation is often blurred. One criterion is whether the research is designed to shape a product or intervention that is still being developed (formative) or a product or intervention that is basically complete and static (summative). The blurring occurs when an intervention that was thought to be static is found to require alterations in order to enhance its impact; the so-called summative evaluation may then be invalidated or become a formative tool guiding modification of the intervention.

Product Development: Formative Evaluation. Today, we see formative evaluation being used in the development not only of educational products but also of such products as smart cards and management information systems (Kerns, 1983). The formative evaluation model was brought to its highest art form in what is referred to as the *CTW model,* referring to Children's Television Workshop where it was developed. As described by Lesser (1975), this model entails a team effort among television producers, content specialists, psychologists, and evaluators. In the development of instructional television, formative evaluation is a well-defined process that clearly defines the roles of evaluators and other team members.

The same cannot be said about formative evaluation of the new technologies. There are two reasons for this. First, many new products require different types of team members. For example, the CTW model required identifying a unique type of television producer who both understood the techniques of orchestrating the video machine and appreciated the contributions that educators and evaluators could make to a product that had to both entertain and teach. Among computer programmers, the parallel to television's producers, there is no tradition of working together in a coordinated fashion with content specialists and instructional designers.

Second, new hardware and software can be very complex, as microcomputer software and videodiscs show, and this complexity creates problems. The microcomputer makes a new kind of educational programming possible. As long as the educational product was linear, as it was in film and television, it was relatively simple to imagine what the finished product might look like at various stages of development and to conduct evaluation on it. Script review, storyboard design, and other features allowed various individuals to imagine what the finished product would look like and to critique it. In contrast, as many participants in the development of computer software have attested, the new interactive products make it almost impossible to visualize what the final product will look like. How does one visualize the twenty or more branching possibilities that a learner can follow in the course of interactive instruction? This issue is particularly salient in the production of videodisc products, because it is impossible to edit and change the videodisc after it has been pressed. In contrast, instructional television producers have been known to make last-minute edits right up to broadcast time.

A related challenge comes from critiquing design prospectuses for microcomputer software. Microcomputer programs are typically interactive text, and each frame on the screen must stand by itself. Therefore, it is necessary for the critic to envision every screen. With instructional television, where the educational messages are imbedded in interesting stories, one can provide a storyboard and the critic can picture how it will look when dramatically acted out. This is easily done because critics have experience with how televised stories look. A single sketch can stand for two to five minutes of video time. Some of the video time can contain educational content, while the rest can be sheer entertainment. In other words, there is room for error when creating educational television, partly because viewers can attend intermittently to the television stimulus and still remain basically attentive to the messages in a fifteen- or thirty-minute production. What happens with microcomputer programs? Here, the learner interacts with each frame to determine what the next frame is going to look like, because it is based on his or her response. If two or three frames in a row present incongruities or if the responses they require are not sufficiently challenging, the learner cannot press a "fast-forward" switch; he or she is likely instead to turn off the machine and leave the entire process. Some people in the field argue that a better and tighter formative evaluation process would solve the problem, but this is not obvious. Cognitive complexity in the design of these new products may require expert judgment to replace the formative strategy of educational television in which first a concept, then a script, then a film segment is tested with a group of test subjects. How is expert judgment to be developed? Expert judgment can be developed by evaluating completed products for lessons about the creation of a next generation of products. The typical strategies now being used involve case studies, in which observers see how learners interact with materials (Yoder, 1983; Williams and others, 1983; Bruce and Starr, 1983). Most of the studies just cited use case study approaches to watch how learners interact with materials. This approach can be extremely useful to find out how hardware and software factors influence user responses to programs. The challenge is to develop a set of guidelines for the creation of new products. Davis (1983) provides an example.

Another issue raised by work on videodiscs at Digital Equipment Corporation relates to the formal features of information technology displays (Ehrlich, 1983). The new technologies have the capacity to present graphic information in multiple colors and text in multiple font styles. It is appropriate to raise the question whether features of the textual and graphic presentation on microcomputer screens can affect learners' grasp of the material or focus their attention on the task at hand. Formal features analysis in television has a long history. Salomon (1979) showed a relationship between the way a camera captured a scene (close-in versus wide-angle) and what children learned. A number of attempts have been made to determine whether presenting instructional television materials in black-and-white or in color makes a difference, but no convincing difference has been shown. It is unlikely that formative research on a single project will shed much light on appropriate use of colors and type fonts. In this area, too, a program of basic research on perception that uses completed instructional programs may be appropriate (Johnston and Ettema, in press).

Impact of Technology: Summative Evaluation. Summative evaluation questions can have a narrow or broad focus. Product testing takes a relatively narrow look at the impact of a new innovation. It asks such questions as, Does the innovation get used? By whom? For what purposes? Do those who interact with the hardware and software as intended achieve the intended outcome; that is, do they acquire new information, complete a bank transaction, or retrieve information of interest? Assessment of the social impact of a technology is a broad issue. The relevant question is how the way of conducting business differs as a result of using the new technology to conduct it. Is the organization somehow more effective, or can it deliver a product more efficiently as a result of the new technology? Those who would assess the impact of new technology on organizational functioning or product delivery should keep four issues in mind.

Specification of the Intervention. The first issue concerns how the technology functions. It is commonplace to talk in global terms about computers or about how computers are taking over functions within an organization. But, if we are to know what to research, the exact way in which the computers are functioning must be specified. For example, microcomputers can be used in schools in at least three different ways, as the title of Taylor's book, *The Computer in the School: Tutor, Tool, Tutee,* captures. In the tutorial mode, students use microcomputers for drill and practice; the microcomputer and appropriate software ask questions and provide feedback on the accuracy of students' answers. When the computer is a tutee, the student learns to program the computer in order to accomplish the student's own goals. Papert (1980) argues that this is the most powerful way in which a microcomputer can be used educationally. When the microcomputer functions as a tool, it is loaded with software for word processing, accounting, and other functions. Similar differentiations can be made regarding the use of computers in business settings. Perhaps the tool aspects of microcomputers are what current advertising most emphasizes. Computers will accomplish a great deal in keeping track of clients, finances, and other aspects of work flow. However, the same computers can also be used for electronic communication with message systems and computer conferencing. The point is that the functionality of the computer needs to be specified carefully, because it is this functionality that is assessed, not some global concept titled *computers.*

Pervasiveness and Substitution. The second issue involves the extent to which the new technology substitutes for old functions. The more extensive the substitution, the greater the possible impact. In a recent study, Schwartz and others (1983) asked what impact microcomputers had on preschool education. While the question was framed broadly, the intervention was not. Preschoolers were allowed to "paint" with a microcomputer and joy stick for a few minutes every day. In contrast, Digital Equipment Corporation's Interactive Videodisc Information System is designed to provide all the training for computer repair people in the field (Ehrlich, 1983). Digital is designing software for this integrated microcomputer–videodisc system that will enable learners around the world to study how to repair a Digital computer product; a human instructor is not needed. In the kindergarten example, the microcomputer substituted very little for the wide range of activities that go on in the preschool classroom. In the Digital example, the computer substituted completely for the many different activities entailed in a traditional training program.

The third issue relates to the pervasiveness of computerization within an organization. This dimension is somewhat different from the substitution dimension, because it involves the extent to which performing some processes by computer has had an impact on other human processes in the organization. Often, the technology implemented in one part of the organization has unintended side effects on another part of the organization. A good example is at AT&T (Bush, 1983). There a new computerized information system bypasses repair supervisors in the assignment of repair work and thereby has an impact on the entire organizational structure.

Technology in Context. The fourth issue involves the relationship between the technology and other contextual factors. Technology is designed to accomplish particular ends. For example, instructional television is designed to convey particular messages to viewers. We know that many aspects of the environment can change what a learner takes away from such an experience. This is nowhere better illustrated than in Sanders's recent paper (1983); he catalogues the ways in which the impact of the television series "ThinkAbout" was drastically altered by teachers, students, organizational factors, and other contextual factors beyond the control of the technology itself. Char (1983) makes the same point regarding the multimedia production "Voyage of the Mimi." A similar case can be made for teletext (see Chapter Two). Since the role of context in mediating the effects of technologies has only recently attracted research attention, there is a paucity of firm principles to guide research efforts.

Research Methods

Natualistic Observation and Case Studies. What is needed before adequate studies of the impact of technology can be designed is greater use of naturalistic observation and case studies to develop hypotheses about how technology interacts with users and context. Naturalistic observation of selected cases or phenomena has become popular in recent years (Yin, 1981). Adopted partly in response to the known limitations of large-scale survey research, the techniques of naturalistic observation have provided an understanding of complex social phenomena that was not possible with the abstractions of questionnaire items completed by respondents who were heavily involved in the situation under study. Naturalistic observation can be used in both exploratory and confirmatory studies. In confirmatory studies, the observer uses protocols or observation guides across a sampling of events to look for patterns or confirming hypotheses about interrelationships. In exploratory studies, the observer must be creative in looking for new ways to interpret old realities.

With the new technologies, both exploratory and confirmatory studies are needed to capture the complex ways in which technology, context, and users interact. The "ThinkAbout" case studies show how good exploratory ethnography can help us to understand how technology affects users. Sanders (1983) summarizes these ethnographies. For years, the literature on instructional television has made the implicit assumption that the individual viewer should learn as much as the show contains, mediated only by attention and comprehension factors in the individual. The ethnographers in the "ThinkAbout" studies discovered a number of contextual factors that limited the impact of the series on students who were exposed to it — factors that probably limit the impact of any educational technology used in a classroom setting. These factors included competing curricular goals, a pace of instruction that interfered with accomplishment of goals advocated in the television series, the quality of the television signal, classroom interruptions, teacher competence with the material being taught, the view (shared by many teachers) that use of media is incompatible with quality instruction, teachers' use of students' viewing time as a teaching break, and students' perception of television time as break time. It is very difficult for social science to assess these factors with traditional paper-and-pencil questionnaire methods, whether respondents are teachers or students. In a similar fashion, the methods of natural field observation may be required if we are to understand the ways in which any of the new information technologies are interacting with users and contexts. Clearly, the strength of natural field observation lies in the richness of the data, which could not be collected by other methods. Case studies have their weaknesses as well. They sample a limited number of occurrences. Although the detail is rich, one sees events in only a limited number of settings. How does one know whether or not the settings chosen are representative? These questions frequently argue for the combination of case study with methods associated with large-scale surveys. Johnston and his colleagues (1984) provide an example of this combination. Case studies also present problems of cost and timeliness. They are costly because they are so labor-intensive, and they often require much more time for data collection than surveys do.

One innovative approach to case studies use video case studies. In Chapter Three, Henry Ingle describes how this approach was used to study the use of microcomputers in public schools. The strategy was to develop a conceptual scheme well in advance of data collection. The researchers then contracted the districts to be studied to discuss the kinds of information that would be collected. The researchers' presence was brief by most standards for case studies — three days in each district. But, the same data were collected from all the districts studied. Then, a team of twenty-five experts viewed all the videotapes and worked out a consensus interpretation. This consensus made it possible to edit the twenty hours of videotape into four thirty-minute summary tapes. Ingle provides a good example of how a new technology can be used to gather the kind of data needed to understand new technology.

Product Testing. As technologies stabilize and as their use becomes routine, the need to test the efficacy of some technologies will arise. Market performance will not provide sufficient justification for some stakeholder groups. For example, management at AT&T wanted evidence that the computerized repair order system was cost-beneficial (Bush, 1983). The technologies for which accountability is most likely to be demanded in the future are those purchased with public funds. Technologies designed to teach will be among them, because they are candidates for adoption in public education. Technologies in this class include educational applications of microcomputers, videodiscs, and teletext. But, even after a technology becomes stable, the character described for it by designers is likely to undergo some change when it is placed in the hands of users. Hall and others (1975) point out how new educational programs are seldom implemented as their designers intend until the implementers have used the programs for several years. Even then, they document, the innovation is likely to be altered in ways that the designers did not intend. Historically, this phenomenon has led to weak tests of the effectiveness of new educational programs and products and to failure to disentangle a product's potential from problems of training and implementation. One solution to the problem is the *product validation* approach described by Johnston (1981). Adopters are specially trained to approximate the kind of use expected after two or three years of normal dissemination, adoption, and adaptation. A traditional pretest-to-posttest design is used to assess growth and change, but the quality and quantity of implementation are carefully documented and incorporated into the analysis. This approach draws on strategies developed for the assessment of medical technologies, and it shows how traditional educational evaluation strategies need to be adapted to fit the intervention being evaluated.

Program evaluation is rooted in a tradition of collecting social science data for use in decision making. Over the years, it has well served our needs to assess the quality of educational products, social programs, and medical technologies. Evaluators have responded to the needs of various stakeholders for useful information by adapting traditional social science research strategies. As evaluators turn their attention to information technologies, additional adaptation is needed. The value of the studies yet to be performed rests on the creativity of evaluators in shaping their craft to the characteristics of the new object of inquiry and to the needs of new stakeholders.

References

Bruce, B., and Starr, K. "Microcomputers in the Classroom: Changes in the Writing Process." Paper presented at the annual meeting of the Evaluation Research Society, Chicago, October 1983.

Bush, R. "Evaluating the Impact of New Computer Technologies in the Telephone Industry." Paper presented at the annual meeting of the Evaluation Research Society, Chicago, October 1983.

Char, C. "Formative Research in the Creation of Educational Software for Children." Paper presented at the annual meeting of the Evaluation Research Society, Chicago, October 1983.

Crane, V. "Content Development for Children's Television Programs." In E. L. Palmer and A. Dorr (Eds.), *Children and the Faces of Television: Teaching, Violence, Selling*. New York: Academic Press, 1980.

Davis, B. G. "Testing New Products: Interactive Videodiscs." Paper presented at the annual meeting of the Evaluation Research Society, Chicago, October 1983.

Ehrlich, L. R. "Testing Competencies Using a Computer-Based Interactive Video System." Paper presented at the annual meeting of the Evaluation Research Society, Chicago, October 1983.

Hall, G. E., Loucks, S. F., Rutherford, W. L., and Newlove, B. W. "Levels of Use of the Innovation: A Framework for Analyzing Innovation Adoption." *Journal of Teacher Education*, 1975, 26 (1), 52-56.

Johnston, J. "Evaluation of Curriculum Innovations: A Product Validation Approach." In C. B. Aslanian (Ed.), *Improving Educational Evaluation Methods: Impact on Policy*. Beverly Hills: Sage, 1981.

Johnston, J., and Ettema, J. "Using Television to Best Advantage: Research for Prosocial Television." In J. B. Bryant and D. Zilman (Eds.), *Perspectives on Media Effects*. Hillsdale, N.J.: Erlbaum, in press.

Johnston, J., Luker, R., and Mergendoller, J. *Micros in the Middle School: A Snapshot in 1984*. Bloomington, Ind.: Agency for Instructional Technology, 1984.

Kerns, K. "Formative Evaluation to Develop 'Smart Cards.'" Paper presented at the annual meeting of the Evaluation Research Society, Chicago, October 1983.

Lesser, G. S. *Children and Television: Lessons from Sesame Street*. New York: Vintage Books, 1975.

Papert, S. *Mindstorms: Children, Computers, and Powerful Ideas*. New York: Basic Books, 1980.

Rice, R. E., and Borgman, C. "The Use of Computer-Monitored Data in Information Science and Communication." *Journal of the American Society for Information Science*, 1983, 34, 247-256.

Salomon, G. *Interaction of Media, Cognition, and Learning: An Exploration of How Symbolic Forms Cultivate Mental Skills and Affect Knowledge Acquisition*. San Francisco: Jossey-Bass, 1979.

Sanders, J. R. "The Importance of Context When Studying the Impact of Instructional Television." Paper presented at the annual meeting of the Evaluation Research Society, Chicago, October 1983.

Schwartz, S., Rivkin, M., and Wilson, J. "The Introduction of Microcomputers into the Preschool Classroom." Paper presented at the annual meeting of the Evaluation Research Society, Chicago, October 1983.

Taylor, R. P. (Ed.). *The Computer in the School: Tutor, Tool, Tutee*. New York: Teachers College Press, 1980.

Williams, D. D., Quinn, W., and Gale, L. E. "Evaluating the Use and Effectiveness of Student-Controlled Interactive Videodiscs." Paper presented at the annual meeting of the Evaluation Research Society, Chicago, October 1983.

Yin, R. K. "The Case Study as a Serious Research Strategy." *Knowledge: Creation, Diffusion, Utilization,* 1981, *3,* 97–114.

Yoder, E. "Evaluating an Evolving Computer-Aided Management System." Paper presented at the annual meeting of the Evaluation Research Society, Chicago, October 1983.

Jerome Johnston is associate research scientist at the Institute for Social Research at the University of Michigan.

Index

A

AGRI-DATA, 7
Albany, Ohio, microcomputers in, 47-48
Ann Arbor, Michigan, microcomputers in, 47-48
Association for Educational Communications and Technology (AECT), 51
AT&T, 77, 83, 85
Austria, teletext in, 24

B

Bank Street College, Center for Children and Technology at, 44
Becker, H. J., 54, 69
Bernard, H., 61, 69
Blundell, G., 54, 69
Borgman, C., 61, 70, 78, 86
Bostrom, R., 62, 69
Brady, M., 46, 51
Bruce, B., 81, 86
Bryk, A. S., 63, 69
Bush, R., 77, 83, 85, 86

C

Campbell, D., 71
Canada, teletext in, 25
Carey, J., 2, 7, 21, 23-41
Case, D., 58, 59, 66, 67, 70
Case studies: of new media, 57-58; for technology evaluation, 80-81, 83-85; videotape, 43-51
Cellular radio. *See* New media
Champness, B., 31, 40
Chandler, J., 61, 69
Dhange, kinds of, and new media, 65
Char, C., 83, 86
Chen, T. C., 5, 21
Chervany, N., 61, 63, 69
Children's Television Workshop (CTW), 77, 79
Christie, B., 71
Cincinnati, Ohio, microcomputers in, 47-48
Clarke, P., 7, 21
Communication satellites. *See* New media
Compaine, B. M., 5, 21
CompuServe, 54, 55
Computer conferencing, as new media, 53, 55, 58, 59-60, 61, 64-65, 67
Computers. *See* Microcomputers; Personal computers
Confidentiality, and computer-monitored data, 62
Corporation for Public Broadcasting (CPB), 25, 26
Crane, V., 74, 86
Cummings, T., 62, 69
Cupertino, California, microcomputers in, 47-48

D

D'Alessio, D., 69
Danowski, J., 61, 69
Davis, B. G., 81, 86
De Alberdi, M., 31, 40
Dervin, B., 8, 21
DIALOG, 56
Diaries, for field trials, 37-38
Digital Equipment Corporation, 81, 82
Dominick, W., 61, 70
Dow Jones News Retrieval, 54
Dozier, D., 8, 21

E

Ehrlich, L. R., 81, 82, 86
Electronic mail, as new media, 53, 55, 57-58, 59, 64, 66, 68
Elton, M., 2, 23-41
ERIC, 56
Ethnography: in technology evaluation, 84; and teletext, 29-30
Ettema, J. S., 1-2, 5-21, 55, 70, 74-75, 78, 81, 86
Europe, teletext in, 24-25
Evaluation: with computer-monitored data, 60-62, 78; concept of, 74-75; criteria of, 63-64; design and method

Evaluation *(continued)*
  of, for videotex, 11–12; domain of, 64–65; implications of new media characteristics for, 56–68; methods of, 65; of microcomputers, 43–51; of new media, 53–71; of new technologies, 73–87; and simultaneity of influence, 67–68; stakeholders for, 63; of teletext, 23–41; of videotex, 5–21

F

Fairfax County, Virginia, microcomputers in, 47–48
Fargo, North Dakota, videotex in, 7–20
Federal Communications Commission (FCC), 25, 37
Field experiment, and teletext, 27
Field studies: design implications for, 37–38; expanded, 30–31; implementation and findings of, 31–32; laboratory study compared with, 26, 40; lessons about, 38–40; logic of, 8; multiple measures in, 39–40; pilot, 29–30; of teletext, 23–41; of videotex, 5–21
Fink, E., 65, 71
First Bank System, videotex of, 5–21
FirstHand, prototype users of, 5–21
Formative evaluation: concept of, 78–79; for technologies, 74, 79–81
France, teletext in, 25
Frost F., 71

G

Gale, L. E., 86
Giuliano, V., 67, 69
Grayson, L. P., 43, 51
Greenberg, B., 69
Grove, J., 71

H

Halamaj, J., 67, 70
Hall, G. E., 85, 86
Hamilton, S., 61, 63, 69
Hannan, M., 65, 69
Head Start, 74
Heeter, C., 61, 69
Heinen, J., 62, 69
Hewes, D., 65, 69

Hiemstra, G., 61, 69
Hiltz, S. R., 59, 60, 61, 66, 67, 69, 70
Hirsch, P., 69, 70
Howard, G., 71

I

Information retrieval systems. *See* New media
Ingle, H. T., 2–3, 43–51, 84–85
Interactive cable. *See* New media
Interdependencies, and technology evaluation, 77
International Communication Association, 56
International Data Corporation, 55, 70
Irving, R., 40

J

Johansen, R., 59, 70
Johns Hopkins University, microcomputer surveys by, 44
Johnston, J., 1–4, 55, 70, 73–87

K

Katzman, N., 10, 21
Kerns, K., 74, 79, 86
Kerr, E., 60, 70
Killworth, P., 69
Kincaid, L., 60, 70
Kline, F. G., 7, 8, 21
Kling, R., 68, 70
Knowledge Industry Publications, 54, 70

L

Laboratory studies: field studies compared with, 26, 40; for teletext, 30, 31
LaRose, R., 71
Ledingham, J., 8, 21
Lesser, G. S., 79, 86
Lippitt, M., 67, 70
Loucks, S. F., 86
Lucas, W., 26, 40
Luker, R., 86

M

McVoy, D., 69
Magazine Index, 55–56

Management Contents, 55-56
Market Data Retrieval, 44
Market information videotex for, 5-21
Martin, J., 5, 21
Maryland Instructional Television Center, 48
Maxwell, S., 71
Media. *See* New media
Mergendoller, J., 86
Meters, for field trials, 37
Microcomputers: appropriateness of, for evaluation, 44-46; results of, 45; and technology evaluation, 79-80, 82; video case study of, 43-51
Miller, J., 67, 70
Monetary Deregulation and Control Act of 1980, 6
Monge, P., 65, 70

N

National Institute of Education, 74
National Science Foundation, 5, 23*n*, 26, 74
National Telecommunications and Information Administration (NTIA), 25, 26
National Weather Service, 32
Naturalistic observation, in technology evaluation, 83
Netherlands, teletext in, 24
New media: analysis of, 53-71; characteristics of, 56-68; and communication processing, 59-60; computer-monitored data on, 60-62; concept of, 53-54; and control group, 66; diffusion of, 53-56; early adoption and innovation of, 66-67; and kinds of change, 65; literature on, 55-56; network analysis of, 60, 65; newness of, 56-59; numbers of, 54-55; research theories and approaches for, 55, 58; and simultaneity of influence, 67-68; social presence of, 58-59; stakeholders for, 63; summary on, 68-69; as systems, 62-65; task content of, 58-59
New York University, Alternate Media Center at, 25
Newlove, B. W., 86
Nielsen, A. C., 54, 70
Norman, A. R. D., 5, 21

North Dakota, videotext prototype in, 7-20
North Dakota State University, extension services of, 7

O

Office information systems, as new media, 53, 58, 64, 65, 66, 67
Office of Technology Assessment, 43, 44, 51
Orlando, Florida, teletext in, 24

P

Paisley, W., 10, 21, 57, 66, 70
Palmer, E., 55, 70
Panko, R., 55, 70
Papert, S., 82, 86
Penney Company, J. C., 7
Penniman, W., 61, 70
Personal computers, as new media, 53, 54, 55, 58, 68
Pillsbury Company, 7
Plains, Montana, microcomputers in, 47-48
Product validation, and technology evaluation, 85
Project BEST (Basic Education Skills through Technology), 43-51
Prototype users, of videotex, 5-21
Public information, teletext for, 23-41

Q

Quantum Science Corporation, 55, 70
Quick, S., 26, 40
Quinn, W., 86

R

Reliability, for video case study, 49
Rice, R. E., 3, 8, 21, 53-71, 78, 86
Richards, W., 60, 70
Rivkin, M., 86
Robinson, K., 5, 21
Rogers, E., 28, 41
Rogers, E. M., 60, 67, 70
Russell, J., 54, 70
Rutherford, W. L., 86

S

Sailor, L., 69
Salomon, G., 81, 86
San Diego, California, teletext in, 24
Sanders, J. R., 83, 84, 86
Sandler, C., 55, 71
Schwartz, R., 71
Schwartz, S., 82, 86
Scriven, M., 78
Sechrest, L., 71
Shinn, A., 26, 41
Short, J., 58, 71
Siegeltuch, M., 30, 40
Sigel, E., 5, 7-8, 21
Smith, A., 5, 21
Social Science Citation Index, 55-56
Sociological Abstracts, 55-56
Source, The, 54, 55
Stakeholders: implications of videotex for, 17-20; for new media, 63; for technology evaluation, 74-75; for teletext research, 25-26
Starr, K., 81, 86
Strassman, P., 67, 71
Summative evaluation: concept of, 79; for technologies, 74, 81-83
Sweden, teletext in, 24

T

Tapscott, D., 65, 66, 71
Taylor, R. P., 82, 86
Technology evaluation: analysis of, 73-87; attributes of, 76-78; audiences for, 74-76; background on, 73-74; and context, 83; on impact of technology, 81-83; and nonlinearity, 77-78; and pervasiveness, 82-83; for product development, 79-81; for product testing, 85; research methods for, 83-85; and self-monitoring, 78; and specification of intervention, 81-82; strategies of, 78-83; and substitution, 82
Teletext: access time for, 36; advantages and disadvantages of, 24; analysis of, 23-41; content production for, 32-33; design implications for, 35-40; findings on, 31-35; medium of, 23-25; as new media, 53; production costs for, 35-36; research issues for, 26-28; research plan for, 28-31; service format for, 33-35; and stakeholders, 25-26; and technology evaluation, 73
Terborg, J., 65, 71
Time, Inc., 24
Turoff, M., 59, 59

U

United Kingdom, teletext in, 24, 25, 38
U.S. Department of Agriculture, 66
U.S. Department of Education, 43, 47
U.S. Department of Health, Education, and Welfare, 26

V

Valley City, North Dakota, videotex in, 7-20
Vertical blanking interval (VBI), and teletext, 23, 24
Video case studies: advantages of, 46-47, 50; analysis of, 43-51; background on, 43-44; conclusions on, 50-51; process of, 47-48; research topics for, 44-45; strategy for, 48-50; for technology evaluation, 84-85
Videodisc: as new media, 53; and technology evaluation, 73, 80, 81
Videotex: analysis of, 5-21; background on, 5-6; developer's stake in, 6-9, 17-19; evaluation of, 11-17; impact of, 9-11; implications of, for stakeholders, 17-20; and information equity, 10-11, 19-20; market for technology of, 6-9; as new media, 53, 54, 55, 58, 66, 68; society's stake in, 9-11, 17, 19-20; and system as concept, 8, 12-14, 18; and system in prototype, 8-9, 14-17, 18, 19; and technology evaluation, 73, 74-75; usage records for, 15; user evaluation of, 16-17

W

Wahpeton, North Dakota, videotex in, 7-20
Washington, D.C., teletext in, 35-40
Webb, E., 61, 71
Weick, K., E, 46, 51
Wilkinson, L. C., 46, 51
Williams, D. D., 81, 86
Williams, E., 71

Williams, F., 55, 71
Williams, R., 6, 21
Wilson, J., 86
Woelfel, J., 65, 71
Word processing, as new media, 53, 55, 57, 64, 67

Y

Yin, R. K., 83, 87
Yoder, E., 81, 87
Young, A., 65, 69